BETTER HOMES AND GARDENS®

BULBS

FOR ALL SEASONS

BETTER HOMES AND GARDENS® BOOKS
Des Moines

MEREDITH® BOOKS
President, Book Group: Joseph J. Ward
Vice President and Editorial Director: Elizabeth P. Rice
Art Director: Ernest Shelton

Better Homes and Gardens®
BULBS FOR ALL SEASONS
Editor: Douglas A. Jimerson
Art Director: Brad L. Ruppert
Senior Editor: Marsha Jahns
Writer: Karen Weir-Jimerson
Photographers: Peter Krumhardt, Bill Stites
Illustrator: Gary Palmer
Regional Editor: Bonnie Maharam
Copy Editors: Durrae Johanek, Kay Sanders, and David Walsh
Electronic Production Coordinator: Paula L. Forest
Indexer: Sharon Novotne O'Keefe

Special thanks:
•International Flower Bulb Information Center—Annet Scheeren, Frans Roozen,
Grace Holt, Warre de Vroe, and Jacqueline van der Kloet
•The Netherlands Flower Bulb Information Center—Sally Ferguson and Judy Sloate
•Conni Cross

MEREDITH CORPORATION CORPORATE OFFICERS:
Chairman of the Executive Committee: E.T. Meredith III
Chairman of the Board, President and
Chief Executive Officer: Jack D. Rehm
Group Presidents:
Joseph J. Ward, Books
William T. Kerr, Magazines
Philip A. Jones, Broadcasting
Allen L. Sabbag, Real Estate
Vice Presidents:
Leo R. Armatis, Corporate Relations
Thomas G. Fisher, General Counsel and Secretary
Larry D. Hartsook, Finance
Michael A. Sell, Treasurer
Kathleen J. Zehr, Controller and Assistant Secretary

introduction

Creating gorgeous gardens with flowering bulbs is easy because no other

group of plants has so much to offer. Bulbs have it all: vibrant color, exotic flower form,

hardy character, and astounding versatility. First to bloom in late winter and last

to close in autumn, there are even bulb species that you can force indoors during

the winter. BULBS FOR ALL SEASONS is your one-stop information source for

planting, care, and gardening with flowering bulbs. For each season, major bulbs are listed

in alphabetical order, followed by exciting lesser-known bulbs. And, for easy reference,

all information about a specific bulb is listed in one place: best-pick species and varieties,

planting instructions, seasonal care and tips, and ideas for stunning garden placement.

This book's inspired landscape and garden plans combined with its practical advice about

growing bulbs will help you become a successful full-season bulb gardener.

table of contents

bulb gardens

The universal appeal of bulbs is evident in the noblest and the most humble gardens throughout the world. The reason for their wide popularity is that bulbs attract gardeners on so many different levels. For the penny-wise gardener, bulbs provide an inexpensive and long-term investment in the beauty of their yard. For the dreamer, bulbs have starring roles in the mystical play of seasons: a play in four acts, each season with its major and minor players, some who garner center stage and others content to rest in the footlights. For all gardeners, bulbs have the traits they strive to find for their gardens—bulbs are practical, hardy, and, above all, generous bloomers.

Year in and year out, flowering bulbs provide constant color in any landscape. Important players in garden design, bulbs offer dazzling colors, a smorgasbord of flower types, and nonstop bloom from early spring through frost. Few flowers mark the seasons as well as bulbs; who can think of spring without also envisioning crocus and narcissus, or summertime gardens without the ever-present gladiolus and dahlias. Regardless of the season or geographic location, there are bulb species that will flourish in your garden.

Among the easiest types of garden plants to grow and care for, bulbs perform their wondrous magic with a minimum of attention. Once planted, many bulbs return each year, some multiplying and spreading with great enthusiasm. By selecting the right species from a huge cast of star

The bulb gardening season is off and running when early birds such as galanthus, crocus, and eranthis, below, start to bloom. Plant these little charmers under trees or naturalize them in your lawn. Later, tulips, narcissus, hyacinths, and muscari, right, provide the next wave of color.

bloomers, you can ensure that your garden is alive with constant bloom.

Hardy spring-flowering bulbs emerge just as the snow melts from garden beds, lawns, and woodlands. The bonanza of spring bloom begins with early risers like galanthus, crocus, species tulips, and narcissus. Good locations for these early birds include dooryard and entry gardens, flower beds, and shrub borders. Bulbs also can brighten unexpected spots along fences, be naturalized in your lawn, or be planted under deciduous trees where they'll put on their show before the trees leaf out and shade the area. Latecomers such as *Fritillaria imperialis*, muscari, and late-blooming tulips continue the razzle-dazzle through May. From bright primary colors to sub-

With careful planning, bulbs help keep your garden colorful from spring until fall. In this garden, left, drifts of tulips, narcissus, muscari, and hyacinths flower from April until June. By midsummer, above, the spring bulbs have faded, but the garden is still colorful thanks to a mass planting of orange tuberous begonias mixed with perennials and annuals.

tle pastels, you can mix and match blooms to complement one another. Bulbs planted en masse make the biggest impression, so be generous when you plant. For larger bulbs such as tulips, hyacinths, and daffodils, set in at least a dozen per spot. For small bulbs such as crocus and muscari, plant 50 or more bulbs per clump.

As spring fades into summer, tulips and narcissus give way to warm-weather favorites. Summer-blooming bulbs pick up the pace with the largest selection of species of any season. Exotic, large, bright, and flamboyant, summer bulbs fill your garden to the point of excess. Dinnerplate-sized dahlias, towers of lilies, and crowded cascades of tuberous begonias clamber for space in garden beds. Growing shoulder to shoulder with perennials or bursting

When planning your bulb garden be sure to place the plants where you can enjoy them the most. The extraordinary streetside garden above puts on a traffic-stopping display every May. On a front porch, right, potted bulbs are a natural. Here, tuberous begonias bloom all summer long.

out of containers and window boxes, summer bulbs are lavish in their color and generous in their bloom. As you do with spring bulbs, always be sure to coordinate complementary colors and heights.

Autumn brings a new wave of blooming bulbs. Fall bulbs, such as Oriental lily, lycoris, and sternbergia, rise with the same sense of joy and renewal as their spring counterparts, extending your garden's brilliance. Some fall-blooming species are so hardy they hold their bloom even after the first snow.

As winter descends, the outdoor garden flowers bow to cool weather. Only flowering bulbs offer you the chance to continue your garden indoors with many varieties that you can force during the winter. Quick-to-flower paperwhites and amaryllis offer immediate satisfaction while you chill pots of crocus, tulips, muscari, and hyacinths for late-winter indoor color. By the time your potted bulbs stop blooming, the spring cycle has begun.

Hot late-summer weather won't stop bulbs such as Asiatic and Oriental lilies from putting on a dazzling display. In the late-summer border left, both types of lilies join forces with perennial favorites. Enchantment lilies, below, are magnificent in June alongside coreopsis and heliopsis.

Just because the ground is frozen is no reason to give up bulb gardening. There are many species and varieties that you can force for flowers during the darkest days of winter. Some of the best bulbs for forcing include narcissus, hyacinth, muscari, crocus, and certain tulip varieties. If you don't have the time or space to force bulbs, buy ready-to-bloom amaryllis or paperwhite narcissus.

spring

Rising from the frozen ground each spring, the phoenixlike blooms of spring-flowering bulbs are classic symbols of life's renewal. Whether clumped in formal beds or borders, sprouting at the base of taller trees and shrubs, or popping up in colorful chaos throughout a woodland or lawn, spring-flowering bulbs offer a palette of choices for your landscape. Easy to plant and loyal return visitors, spring gardens literally shout with the colors of old standbys such as crocus, tulip, narcissus, and hyacinth. Yet many lesser-known bulbs, such as scilla, fritillaria, galanthus, and leucojum, rival the hardiness and beauty of their better-known relatives.

allium

When you think of spring-blooming bulbs, alliums may not be the first to come to mind, but don't overlook these dramatic flowers for your spring garden. Planted in groups of three or four, these other-worldly flowers stand tall with singular beauty. Although about 400 species of alliums exist, the best known are edible varieties, which include onions, shallots, leeks, chives, and garlic. While their savory cousins excel in the kitchen, ornamental alliums shine in the perennial bed and border. Their bold and unusual blooms adorn gardens and borders from mid-spring through midsummer.

Alliums show off in a wide range of hues and bloom shapes. Although most alliums fall into varying shades of purple, some varieties bloom in soft pastel hues of blue, pink, yellow, and white. The blooms generally are roundish and are borne on single stems. Leaves grow mostly around the base. Alliums come in all heights, from 4 inches to 4 feet. The flowers range in width from 3 to 12 inches. Tall-grow-

ing species are stunning poking up in the back of perennial borders. Smaller alliums are best suited to rock gardens or the front row of perennial beds. Many alliums hold their bloom for as long as a month, which makes them a sought-after perennial. Some varieties are great naturalizers and will spread generously if allowed to do so.

selecting alliums for your garden

Alliums come in all heights, so you can tuck them in wherever you need a little color in your garden. Here's a list of the most commonly available alliums for your garden:

A. christophii (Stars-of-Persia), Zones 4–9 The late-spring blooms of the stars-of-Persia grow on sturdy

Growing straight and proud, Allium giganteums resemble stately sentries, clad in formal headdress. Sporting magnificent 4-inch lavender flower heads, giant alliums look terrific planted in clumps by themselves, left, or with June-flowering perennials, opposite.

Planted in a sunny location, clumps of drumstick allium, Allium sphaerocephalum, *grow bigger and better every year. In this summer border,
a crowd of drumstick alliums blooms alongside a mass of golden-yellow
rudbeckia. Once planted, both of these reliable plants require little care.*

stalks to heights of 2½ feet. Their blooms are 8- to 12-inch bursts of silvery, lavender flower balls. The heads are excellent for drying.

A. giganteum (Giant allium), Zones 5–8 These tall, lilac-blue alliums look stately in any type of garden. Sporting magnificent softball-sized flower heads, regal 4-foot-tall giant alliums are most attractive when planted in groups of three or four bulbs spaced about 1½ feet apart. Adding color and height, their spectacular blooms rise high above other plants on leafless stalks. Appearing in July, giant alliums are excellent cutting flowers. Cut a few for dried bouquets before the flowers fade. Hang long stalks, heads down, in a dark, well-ventilated place until dry. To keep colors bright, place bouquets away from sunlight.

A. karataviense (Turkestan onion), Zones 4–8 For a shorter allium to tuck into a rock garden or front border, try the 6- to 10-inch-tall *A. karataviense*. The reddish-white blooms are ⅝ inch wide and contrast nicely in a border planting with other late-spring bloomers or do equally well in pots.

A. moly (Golden garlic or lily leek), Zones 3–8 Tiny alliums are at home in front of taller perennials, where they can capture your attention without begging for closer inspection. Short and sweet, 12-inch golden garlic requires strong morning sun and will spread rapidly. Small yellow blooms grace their stems in May and June. These alliums are a good choice for naturalizing.

A. neapolitanum (Daffodil garlic, flowering onion), Zones 7–9 The fragrant, 2- to 3-inch-wide snow-white bloom clusters of the daffodil garlic allium prefer the warmer climates. These spring bloomers require full sun and grow to 14 inches tall. They excel planted in containers. Try a mixture of same-size *A. neapolitanum* and *A. moly* for a yellow and white color mixture.

A. oreophilum, Zones 4–7 The airy, pinkish-purple blooms of *A. oreophilum* appear in late spring on

All alliums, including the A. moly, *above, have similar cultural needs. Sunshine and a reasonably fertile soil that drains well are all you really need to keep your alliums in top form. Because of their pungent fragrance, most species resist attacks by squirrels, mice, and other pests. Once in bloom, allium flowers are long lasting, both on the plant and in a cut bouquet.*

diminutive plants that grow only 4 inches tall. Requiring full sun, these long-lasting alliums are ideal tucked amid a rock garden or in the front of a perennial border.

A. rosenbachianum (Rosenbach onion), Zones 5–8 Cousins to onions, alliums often carry the family name and live up to it. Rosenbach onions release a pungent aroma when cut. Deep violet blooms measure 5 inches across and grow on 2-foot leafless stems. These midsummer bloomers hold their form and color for three to four weeks and are excellent for both cut and dried bouquets.

A. schoenoprasum (Chive), Zones 3–9 An ornamental and edible allium, the chive does double duty in the flower and kitchen garden. Both the flowers and the foliage of chives are as beautiful as they are tasty. Dainty purple-pink flower heads borne on grasslike foliage appear in summer.

A. sphaerocephalum (Drumstick allium, round-headed garlic), Zones 5–9 Allium blossoms, perched atop leafless stalks, appear to float in midair. Swaying in a breezy orbit 2 feet above the earth, the 1-inch reddish-purple blooms of drumstick allium are excellent contrasts for midsummer borders. Eager to naturalize, stunning in a bouquet, and superb as a dried flower, they are a versatile allium choice.

A. ursinum (Bear's garlic, Ramsons), Zones 4–9 Allium bulbs sleep underground until warm weather coaxes them into bloom. Waking from hibernation in summer, bear's garlic creates an uproar with its 2-inch white blossoms. Mass these 18-inch-tall jewels at the edge of a perennial border.

planting and care

Alliums will flourish in any garden location that receives at least six hours of sunlight each day. Because alliums sport heavy blooms on long stems, they do best in borders protected from strong winds. They do well in ordinary garden soil and are easy to grow.

Before planting your bulbs in the fall, improve the soil fertility and drainage with organic matter such as composted manure and sphagnum peat moss. As a general rule, plant the bulbs two times deeper than their diameter (for example, plant a 2-inch bulb 4 inches deep). Allow 4 to 12 inches between bulbs (less for smaller alliums, more for larger bulbs). After planting, water deeply. To insulate the bulbs in winter, cover the bed with a 4-inch-thick mulch of leaves or straw.

Plant large alliums singly or in groups of three to five bulbs.

Mass smaller alliums in clumps of a dozen or more bulbs.

crocus

The lovely blooms of the crocus have heralded the end of winter since antiquity. Native to the Mediterranean region, these plucky favorites are best known for poking their brave buds through the snows of late winter and early spring to spread color and hope throughout woodlands, garden beds, and lawns. About 80 species exist, which allows a large variety of color choices and combinations. Crocus blooms in exquisite shade variations of bright white, buttery yellow, and velvety purple. Striped varieties also exist. Planted during the cool weather of autumn, crocuses return early each spring, blooming at ground level or on tiny stalks. Delicate green and white grasslike foliage surrounds the six-petaled, chalice-shaped flowers, which sustain a bloom for about two weeks. Their name derives from the Greek word *krokos*, which means saffron. Indeed, it is the fall-blooming *Crocus sativus* whose dried stigmas are sold as the costly seasoning and food-colorant saffron, used in Mediterranean and Eastern recipes.

Most gardeners are familiar with the Dutch hybrid *Crocus vernus*. Another, lesser-known group of crocus, called species crocus, is equally wonderful and deserves a place in the garden. Species crocus is smaller than the Dutch hybrids but blooms earlier, most setting forth blooms before the foliage has caught up. Both types of crocus are at their best planted in large drifts or clumps. Their diminutive height of 4 to 6 inches makes crocus a natural understory choice. Try white crocus with yellow species tulips, or purple crocus nestled below red tulips tinged with yellow. Or team crocus with flowering shrubs such as azaleas and rhododendrons to create symphonies of color. If you have the space, set crocus free in a meadow, woodland, or lawn. Crocus is a happy naturalizer and returns for years.

Hybrid crocus and kaufmanniana tulips are a perfect match. Both bloom early in spring and enhance each other when paired in rock gardens or under trees. This stunning garden border, right, contains 'Love Song' tulips and 'Remembrance' crocus. After flowering, the foliage is left on the plant to ripen.

To brighten your spirits on a dreary winter day, consider forcing crocus indoors for winter bloom. For instructions on forcing crocus, see Chapter 5, pages 180 and 181.

selecting crocus for your garden

There are both spring- and fall-blooming crocus species. Spring bloomers appear here. See Chapter 4, page 157, for information on fall-blooming crocus varieties. Here's a list of commonly available crocus for your garden:

C. biflorus (Scotch crocus), Zones 5–9 A popular choice for rock gardens, the lavender-shaded scotch

A garden bursting with 'Jeanne d' Arc' crocuses and 'White Splendor' blanda anemones, above, is so bright the blooms are eye-catching even at night. Tuck these pint-size beauties under trees or in rock gardens.

crocus grows to about 4 inches tall. Some varieties are striped and are stunning planted beside complementary-colored crocus blooming at the same time.

C. chrysanthus (Snow crocus, golden crocus), Zones 4–9 The snow crocus has small blooms and grows to 4 inches tall. Leaves appear after the bloom. An early and colorful spring bloomer, this hardy crocus chases away the last remnants of snow to usher in spring in its vivid shades of yellow, white, and blue. For yellow and purple crocus, try 'E. A. Bowles'; for a pure-white crocus, plant 'Snow Bunting.'

C. tomasinianus (Tomasinian crocus), Zones 4–5 The unusual lavender blooms of this crocus open to a star shape and expose bright orange stigmas. Both leaves and blooms appear at the same time. An early spring flower, it grows to 4 inches tall. This species reproduces quickly.

C. vernus (Dutch or common crocus), Zones 3–9 The most widely cultivated crocus, Dutch crocus is bigger than other varieties. These hardy little bloomers look stunning in clumps of eight to 12 bulbs planted in lawns and grassy areas. Combine the snow-white 'Jeanne d'Arc' with golden-yellow 'Yellow Mammoth,' the lavender-striped 'Pickwick,' and the deep velvet-purple 'Remembrance.'

planting and care

Crocus is grown from small corms planted in late fall. Place corms 2 inches apart, in a hole 2 to 4 inches deep. Top-dress the soil with bonemeal or a balanced fertilizer after planting and each fall for the most abundant bloom. For massive color, plant at least 100 crocus in an area. Because these hardy bulbs are inexpensive and easy to naturalize, the return far exceeds the investment. Crocus multiplies prolifically and you'll be rewarded by large clumps of blooms that increase in size each year.

To ensure the earliest spring bloom, plant crocuses in a sunny, protected spot. Create drifts of color with crocus by digging a winding hole around rocks and shrubs and dropping in handfuls of crocus corms. To mix colors, interplant different colors in the same planting area. Select varieties that have similar bloom times and heights for a uniform look, or plant later-blooming species with early blooming species for time-release color throughout your yard.

Rodents relish the flavor of crocus, so you may have to take preventive measures against marauding pests. To discourage invaders, sprinkle blood meal around the sprouting shoots and repeat after each heavy rain. For best blooms the following year, do not cut or clip the foliage until it is completely withered.

fritillaria

Fritillaria, commonly called fritillary, has been a much maligned plant because one of its more than 100 species emits a musky scent and bears the common name stink lily. Keep in mind, however, that fritillaria is a member of the esteemed lily family. Although the regal crown-imperial is perhaps more odorous than fragrant, you shouldn't judge all fritillaria by this standard. (In fact, the so-called stink lily is a gorgeous plant that commands almost royal attention because of its good looks and patrician stature.) Species of fritillaria range in size and shape from strapping 2- to 4-foot-tall fritillaria to delicate 3- to 6-inch species. Native to Persia, fritillaria sometimes is called Persian lily. An early spring bloomer, fritillaria usually stays in flower for more than two weeks.

selecting fritillaria for your garden

Here's a list of commonly available fritillaria for your garden:

F. imperialis (Crown-imperial), Zones 5–8 The largest of the fritillary family, crown-imperial grows 2 to 4 feet tall and produces 3-inch foliage-capped, nodding, lance-shaped blooms. Although the blooms emit a musky odor, which earned the plant the unpleasant moniker of stink lily, don't let this stigma deter you from including crown-imperial in your garden. Its stellar height and vivid color make it an excellent bedding selection. Planted in groups of three to six plants, the imposing crown-imperial holds court above smaller bulbs. The red-orange variety 'Aurora' is spectacular. 'Lutea,' an all-yellow variety, also is impressive.

F. meleagris (Guinea-hen tulip, checkered lily, snake's-head lily), Zones 4–8 The unusual appearance of this fritillary variety has spawned such descriptive names as guinea-hen tulip (like the mottled feathers of a hen) and snake's-head lily (for its nodding bloom). The Latin word *frillus* means dice cup, which refers to the checkered markings of this species. The 6- to 8-inch-tall plants produce delicate bell-shaped maroon and cream blooms. An excellent rock garden choice, it also naturalizes well. Found in the wild, this species gravitates toward shaded areas and along riverbanks. *F. meleagris* 'Alba' is an all-white variety.

If you're looking for an unusual and dramatic plant for the back of the border, you can't go wrong with Fritillaria imperialis *'Lutea.' Growing 2 feet tall, this golden-yellow plant, right, is a standout, whether planted alone or mixed with its orange-flowering relative, 'Aurora.' It's also believed that the plant's musky-scented bulbs will ward off mice, moles, and other rodents.*

F. michaylowski, Zones 4–9 Growing only 6 to 8 inches tall, the nodding yellow and purple flowers of *F. michaylowski* are a charming addition to any garden. An early spring riser, *F. michaylowski* blooms in sun or partial shade.

F. persica (Fritillaria of Persia), Zones 4–9 The long, straight stems of this fritillary are filled with many bell-shaped brownish-purple flowers. Loving full sun, these plants grow to 30 inches tall. They are magnificent paired with the crown-imperial but are more sweetly fragrant.

planting and care

Fritillaria will flourish in any garden location that receives dappled sunlight or is shaded during the hottest part of the day. Plant fritillary bulbs in autumn as soon as they are available from your garden center because the bulbs tend to dry out quickly. Taller fritillaria, such as crown-imperial and *F. persica*, should be planted 4 to 6

Because fritillaria bulbs dry out, it's important to plant them as soon as you receive them. Add a little bonemeal before planting bulbs.

inches deep in well-drained soil, with 8 inches of space between bulbs. Smaller varieties such as *F. meleagris* should be planted 4 inches deep, with 2 inches between each bulb.

In the spring when the shoots have emerged, fertilize lightly. Fritillaria will bloom best if left undisturbed. Bulbs can be divided after two or three years. Once the blooms are spent, allow the foliage to die back naturally. To propagate, lift and divide the bulbs in the summer by removing the small bulbs from around the large one and replanting.

An early spring bloomer, Fritillaria michaylowski *makes a good companion for other early birds such as anemone, left, and narcissus. Because the flowers are small, you'll get more effect if you plant them in large groupings. They're a good choice for a wooded setting.*

33

hyacinth

The heavily scented, lovely bloom spikes of the hyacinth appear in gardens in early spring. So revered are hyacinths that the Koran says their very blooms feed the soul. Cultivated since Greek and Roman times, the hyacinth received its name from Greek mythology. Apollo named the flower that bloomed from the blood-stained ground where his friend Hyacinthus died. (It's unlikely that the flower described in mythology is the hyacinth we think of today, however.) Regardless, hyacinths are an everlasting tribute to friendship, and complete this role each spring when they return to fill the tired landscape with vibrant blooms. Available in a wide range of colors, you can find hyacinths in shades of blue, pink, purple, white, orange, and yellow. The blooms are extraordinarily fragrant and long lasting, staying in crisp shape for two to three weeks.

Hyacinths are stately, upright plants, and should be planted in clumps or drifts rather than in straight lines to de-emphasize their linear form and to soften their stiff appearance. Because of their uniform height and stocky appearance, hyacinths excel massed in groups in decorative planters or window boxes. Blooming at the same time as narcissus and early blooming tulips, hyacinths are great performers in beds and borders.

No other spring-blooming bulb can match the perfume of the hyacinth, and no other scent so simply whispers of spring. For this reason alone, hyacinths are superb for forcing. See Chapter 5, pages 182 and 183, for instructions on how to force hyacinths.

selecting hyacinths for your garden

All hyacinths that are sold as common garden hyacinths are derived from *Hyacinthus orientalis*. For a dazzling show of robust bloom, try double-

To get the most enjoyment from your hyacinths, plant them near a doorway, along a garden path, or at the edge of a flower border. In this colorful garden, right, 'Pink Perfection,' 'Violet Pearl,' and 'Carnegie' (white) hyacinths team with a crowd of muscari and daffodils.

blooming hyacinth varieties. These produce double florets instead of the single blooms of most hyacinths. Although a bit smaller than their single-blooming relatives, double-blooming hyacinths are extraordinarily colorful and fragrant. Plant 'Hollyhock,' a red variety, or 'Snow Crystal,' a white variety. Here's a listing of commonly available hyacinths for your garden.

Because of their rather stiff nature, hyacinths often look best planted near an architectural element such as a stairway, patio, or driveway. In this entry garden, above, blue and red hyacinths grow amid hostas and two types of narcissus.

H. orientalis (Dutch hyacinth), Zones 4–9 Growing 8 to 12 inches tall, the spiky hyacinth is nearly all bloom. The first year this variety blooms, the spires are magnificent and extremely fragrant. White varieties include 'L'Innocence' and 'Carnegie.' To plant an all-blue garden, select from 'Bismarck,' 'King of the Blues,' 'Delft Blue,' 'Blue Jacket,' and 'Blue Giant.' Red varieties include 'Amsterdam,' 'Hollyhock,' and 'Jan Bos.' For a pastel look, popular pink varieties are 'Pink Pearl' and 'Anna-Marie.' For the velvet richness of purple hyacinths, plant 'Amethyst' and 'Violet Pearl.' The sunny yellow 'City of Haarlem' or the orange 'Gypsy Queen' are fail-safe ways to welcome the warm hues of springtime back to your garden.

H. orientalis albulus (Roman hyacinth), Zones 4–9 A little less military in stature, Roman hyacinths produce delicate multiflowered stems. Available in pink, white, and blue, these hyacinth plants produce spikes that are not as dense as those of *H. orientalis* and are a good choice if your tastes run to less rigid, more diverse blooms. In the garden, Roman hyacinths are a less fussy version of this wonderful garden classic.

planting and care

Hyacinths require full sun, so position them where they'll receive the ample sunlight required for their spectacular bloom. When shopping for bulbs, remember that the bigger the bulb, the bigger the bloom. In early fall, place bulbs in well-drained soil, 5 to 6 inches deep, and allow 5 inches between bulbs. Amend the soil so it is rich in nutrients for a more spectacular bloom show. Although hyacinths are hardy in cold regions, an application of mulch, such as wood chips, helps bulbs overwinter and protects shoots as they push through the soil in the spring.

In their second year, the bulbs split, so the blooms diminish in size. If well fertilized at this time, they'll come back the next year with renewed bloom vigor. If you want the large showy blooms of first-year hyacinths each year, dig up the bulbs after they've flowered and replant them in the fall with new bulbs.

After the bulbs have bloomed and the blossoms are spent, trim the stems but allow the foliage to completely wither before removing or clipping it.

Because hyacinths are susceptible to fungus rot, it's important to plant the bulbs in well-drained soil. Wet soil rots the bulbs, causing the plants to wilt and die. If wet ground is a problem in the location you've chosen, select a different location and replant in the fall with new bulbs.

muscari

Muscari, or grape hyacinths, are as fragrant as they are colorful. Small, vibrant, early spring bloomers, muscari also are wonderfully inexpensive. Best of all, they are long-lived and will bloom for generations. They also spread at will, both by self-seeding and division. Most varieties grow 6 to 8 inches tall and produce spikes of round, closed blooms that resemble bunches of grapes. Muscari bloom in both electric blue and white and hold their colorful place in the garden for up to four weeks. Planted in drifts, their vivid color and oddly formed blooms make an extraordinary carpet beneath early flowering shrubs and trees such as magnolias or flowering crab apples. Planted alone or in tandem with other low-growing species such as dwarf daffodils or anemones, muscari offer you a bold color for your landscape's palette.

As long lasting as a cut flower as it is in the garden, tiny muscari make delicate, diminutive spring bouquets. In addition, they are excellent forcing bulbs. For forcing instructions, see Chapter 5, pages 184 and 185.

selecting muscari for your garden

Here's a list of commonly available muscari for your garden:

M. armeniacum (Armenium grape hyacinth), Zones 5–9 The electric blue color of this small mid-spring bloomer is a wonderful contrast to other bright-blooming bulbs. *M. armeniacum* creates a neon carpet of blue, which offers striking contrast to the peeling white bark of a birch tree or teams perfectly with red tulips and yellow daffodils. Try the vibrant, double-blooming muscari 'Blue Spike.'

M. botryoides (Common grape hyacinth), Zones 4–9 The clustered bloom of this muscari measures ⅛ inch wide and is sweetly fragrant. Use muscari in landscaping, front row borders, and naturalized in and around a woodland. *M. botryoides* 'album' is an all-white variety. Plant bulbs 2 inches apart for best results.

White grape hyacinths, Muscari botryoides 'album,' right, are a little-known relation of the common blue- flowered variety. Plant white grape hyacinths in clumps by themselves or mix them with any of the blue species for contrast. The plants naturalize well, especially in wooded situations and rock gardens.

M. comosum 'plumosum' (Feather hyacinth, Tassel hyacinth), Zones 5–9 The plumelike blooms of these muscari differ greatly from other varieties. They grow 6 to 8 inches tall, and their blooms are gentle lilac mists. Unlike the clumpy grapelike blooms of other muscari, the blooms appear almost shredded. Use these plants in rock gardens and as understory plantings.

M. latifolium, Zones 3–9 This early blooming variety sports two-toned blossoms of blue and purple. The plants grow 4 to 6 inches tall and naturalize well in sun or shade.

planting and care

Once planted, muscari need almost no care. As soon as bulbs become available in garden centers, place them in the ground. Plant 3 inches deep and space 2 to 3 inches apart. These little bulbs produce the best show if planted closely together and in large quantities because these diminutive bulbs produce such small flowers. Muscari thrive in full sun or partial shade, so they do well under trees or shrubs. Rock gardens and borders are ideal locations.

Muscari also naturalize well in short grass. When planting to naturalize, dig a hole 5 inches deep and place the small bulbs 1 to 2 inches apart. After the blooms are spent, allow the leaves to wither before clipping so the bulbs gather strength for next spring's blooming.

Once established, muscari often will send up foliage in the fall but will not bloom until spring.

Eye-catching is the best way to describe the two-toned blooms of Muscari latifolium, *left. This hardy little plant naturalizes well, and once established, will carpet an area with color in just a few years.*

narcissus

If you plant only one bulb in your garden, it should be the cheery narcissus. Stunningly simple and fresh, and nearly always successful, the narcissus has both early and late-blooming varieties. Early narcissus accompanies other season openers such as galanthus, crocus, hyacinths, and species tulips. Late-spring varieties are part of the second wave of color, when tulips also bloom. Because of the wide variety of sizes, the narcissus is ideal in rock gardens, borders and beds, and woodlands.

As many as 26 narcissus species exist, and these lovely beauties go by numerous names, such as daffodil, narcissus, and jonquil. Narcissus was named for the handsome youth in Greek myth who fell in love with his own image and, therefore, is associated with the trait of pride. Indeed, narcissus exudes a sense of exultant display everywhere it blooms.

The narcissus bloom has a trumpet-shaped corona, or cup, surrounded by six petals. The trumpet color often differs from the petal color, which gives the narcissus its perky appearance. Colors range from shades of yellow to orange to pink. By planting both early and late-blooming species, each sustaining blooms for two weeks, you'll enjoy a full month of nodding, dancing narcissus in the yard and in spring bouquets.

Easy to grow and hardy, the narcissus is synonymous with spring. The exotic blooms and lovely tapered foliage make the narcissus a spectacular sight in both beds and borders. It also is a good naturalizers. A wonderland meadow profuse with the nodding heads of narcissus is a lovely sight.

For winter-blooming plants indoors, see Chapter 5, pages 170–175 for forcing instructions.

selecting narcissus for your garden

The narcissus family is divided into 11 classifications based on the flower characteristics and color. Because many catalog and garden centers also follow these categorizations, they'll be helpful in selecting the varieties for your garden. Narcissus grows in Zones 3–9. Here's a list of the classifications and commonly available narcissus for your garden:

Trumpet narcissus Aptly named, trumpet narcissus has a trumpetlike corona (or cup) that extends to a length equal to or longer than the petals that surround it. Growing 16 to 20 inches tall, each stem bears

Synchronize colors, heights, and bloom times when you plant narcissus in your perennial flower garden. In this April garden, right, a background brigade of white 'Thalia' daffodils blooms in precision with pink bleeding-hearts and white arabis. Once the narcissus finishes blooming, you can replant the area with white-blooming annuals such as 'White Porcelain' salvia or white 'Sonata' cosmos.

To imitate the wild, carefree look of a meadow, naturalize clumps of blooming bulbs and wildflowers, such as yellow and white miniature daffodils and wild lilac-blue sweet william.

one flower. Available in pure yellow and snow white, striking bicolor varieties such as the white-petaled, yellow-trumpeted 'Foresight.' All-yellow varieties include 'Unsurpassable' and 'King Alfred,' a favorite in Victorian gardens. For an all-white trumpet daffodil, try 'Mt. Hood' or 'Beersheba.'

Large-cupped narcissus Named for its large cup, which is more than one-third the length of the petals surrounding it, this narcissus has flowers with a corona just a bit shorter than that of a trumpet narcissus. The large-cupped group generally grows about 14 to 20 inches tall and bears one flower per stem. There are wonderful mix-and-match color combinations in this group: 'Amor' is a tricolor beauty with white petals and a showy yellow trumpet rimmed with vivid orange. An unusual and subtle narcissus is the pale pink 'Salomé.' An excellent naturalizer, the all-yellow 'Carlton' blooming along a stream or in a woodland epitomizes spring.

Small-cupped narcissus The small-cupped narcissus has a corona that is less than one-third the length of the petals surrounding it. These smaller-cupped versions come in all the same colors as their larger-cupped cousins and grow to heights of about 14 inches. Try the white-petaled, orange-red–cupped 'Barrett Browning' or the yellow-petaled, orange-cupped 'Birma.'

Double narcissus Unlike the trumpeted narcissus, the double varieties have profusely ruffled centers with several layers of petals. Growing 14 to 18 inches tall, the double narcissus is extraordinary as a cut flower. 'Texas' is a striking yellow-and-orange bicolor beauty.

Cook up your own recipe for spring color by combining clumps of late-blooming yellow narcissus with variegated hostas, left. By the time the narcissus finish blooming, the hostas will have filled out, keeping the garden colorful.

'La Riante' blooms in mid- to late spring in bunches of up to six flowers per 16-inch stem. White petals embrace small, orange cups. Be sure to leave the foliage intact after the plants flower.

Triandrus narcissus Blooming late in the spring, triandrus narcissus is smaller, growing 9 to 14 inches. Gently nodding blossoms make attractive clumps of bloom. Try the all-white 'Thalia' or the lemony 'Hawera.' This narcissus is superb as a forced bulb because of its small size and clustered form.

Cyclamineus narcissus Small, yet sturdy, this group is among the first narcissus to bloom and stands up remarkably well to bad weather. Growing 6 to 10 inches tall, this narcissus is a natural for rock gardens and front border showcasing. Its flowers differ slightly from other narcissus because the petals are reflexed and curved backward, making them look perpetually windswept. Popular varieties include the white-and-yellow 'Beryl' and the vibrant yellows of 'Peeping Tom' and 'February Gold.' The golden-yellow 'Tête-`a-Tête' is spectacular paired with neon-blue muscari.

Jonquilla narcissus The fragrant, small-cupped flowers of *Narcissus jonquilla* are borne on small stems surrounded by reedlike foliage. Stems reach no taller than 12 inches and are covered with clusters of two to six small blooms. Try the all-yellow varieties of 'Sweetness,' 'Baby Moon,' or 'Trevithian,' which is slightly taller and excels as a cut flower.

Tazetta narcissus The oldest narcissus in cultivation, Tazetta narcissus is also a prolific bloomer. Each stem produces a cluster of four to eight perfectly shaped flowers. Long and slender stems grow to 18 inches tall. Sweetly fragrant, Tazetta narcissus is a good naturalizer and the most common choice for forcing. Plant the white-petaled, bright orange trumpet blooms of 'Geranium' in your garden along a walkway or clustered beneath a tree. Bring the extraordinary bloom and fragrance of narcissus indoors to brighten the grayness of winter by forcing paperwhite narcissus or 'Soleil d'Or.'

Poeticus narcissus If you like a narcissus with broad petals and small, delicate trumpets, this is the type for you. Poeticus narcissus has white petals with a small eye of varying colors. 'Actaea' is a popular variety with a striking yellow eye rimmed with a ruffle of red. All blooms of this type of narcissus are very fragrant and are borne on long, elegant stems that reach 18 inches tall, which makes them a premium flower for spring bouquets.

species and wild narcissus

Canaliculatus This smallest of the dwarf species narcissus, it has white petals with a bright, sunny-yellow trumpet.

Obvallaris A golden dwarf narcissus, it loves to naturalize.

Split-corona narcissus Sometimes called butterfly narcissus, this plant has lovely and unusual blooms.

The cup is split and spread open to resemble a beautiful butterfly. Available in yellow, white, and orange, this exotic narcissus is unsurpassed as a cutting flower. Frequently sold in groups of mixed-color assortments, the exotic blooms of the split-corona narcissus will brighten any spring garden. Popular varieties include the bright yellow 'Cassata' and the orange-and-white 'Orangerie.'

planting and care

Narcissus does best in well-drained soil. Before planting your bulbs in the fall, improve the soil fertility and drainage with organic matter such as composted manure and sphagnum peat moss. Narcissus plants are versatile and bloom well in full sun and partial shade, so they can be planted anywhere you need a burst of spring color. Plant narcissus bulbs 4 to 6 inches deep, leaving 3 to 6 inches between bulbs. In warmer climates, you must precool bulbs before planting to ensure optimum bloom. As with most spring-blooming bulbs, allow the leaves to die back before clipping. Daffodils are poisonous and, therefore, are impervious to rodent damage.

naturalizing daffodils

Let Mother Nature be your guide when you plant your spring garden. Instead of limiting bulbs to beds and borders, scatter clumps of daffodils under shrubs, around trees, and in the lawn. This process, called naturalizing, uses natural surroundings as a backdrop for bulb bloom. Eager to spread, daffodils once established soon will populate your landscape, re-creating their original growth in the wild.

Plant clumps of bulbs by digging one large hole. Sprinkle in bonemeal, then plant the bulbs at the right depth.

Naturalize bulbs in open areas by scattering them randomly on top of the ground. Dig a hole for each bulb.

To plant bulbs under trees where roots make digging difficult, use a bulb auger attached to your drill.

tulip

You'd never know from their simple and innocent blooms that the gentle tulip's history reads more like a mystery novel than a botanical journal. Its introduction into the West was fraught with wild financial speculation upon which fortunes were built or broken. Grown in Persia for thousands of years, tulips were introduced to Western culture nearly 400 years ago. These bulbs reputedly were stolen from a botanist in the Netherlands and widely distributed. Whatever their origin, once tulips arrived in Holland, they were there to stay.

By the mid-17th century, the Dutch so loved the beauty of tulips that they triggered a continental craze called tulipomania. The demand for these imports far exceeded the supply, and some rarer varieties were sold for thousands of dollars. The Dutch traded tulips for money, crops, and real estate until the Dutch government finally stepped in to restore order. Although this frantic case of tulip fever cooled, the tulip remains one of the most popular garden flowers—and with good reason. Tulips are hardy, require little care, and bloom for years once established.

Tulips generally are divided into 15 different classes, which vary in appearance and season of bloom. The early bloomers include single early and double early. Mid-season bloomers include mendel, triumph, and darwin hybrid. Late- or May-flowering tulips include darwin, lily-flowered, cottage, rembrandt, parrot, and double late. And for extra-early flowers, there are the species tulips: kaufmanniana, fosterana, greigii, and others.

You can show off tulips alone, or use them to brighten a perennial or shrub border. For a continuous show of color in an all-tulip bed, however, be sure to plant a combination of early, mid-, and late-flowering varieties. Use the early blooming varieties in front of the mid- and late-season tulips, and save the shorter species tulips for the border edge or rock garden.

Imagine a garden bed awash with the elegant pink and white blooms, right, of 'Angelique.' A peony-flowered tulip, this double late variety blooms in May, often alongside its namesake—the true peony. 'Angelique' grows about 20 inches tall. Plant in a sheltered location where the wind won't topple them.

'Olympic Flame,' a darwin hybrid tulip, grows 2 feet tall, producing a spectacular show of yellow-and-red flowers in mid-May. The flowers are larger than average, with very strong stems.

For best results, tulips need a period of cold and darkness to bloom. In northern gardens, plant tulips in the fall before the ground freezes. In southern locations where winter temperatures do not regularly drop below freezing, treat tulips as annuals. You can buy prechilled bulbs and set them out in the spring, or your can buy bulbs eight to 10 weeks before planting time and chill them in your refrigerator.

Tulips grow well in almost any type of soil, but be sure the planting site is well drained. Standing water will rot the bulbs. Tulips also prefer a sunny location, but a spot that receives a little late-afternoon shade will keep the plants blooming longer. To chase away the winter blues, bring some of your bulbs indoors for forced blooming; see Chapter 5, pages 176–179, for instructions.

selecting tulips for your garden

Tulips grow in zones 3–8. Here's a list of commonly available tulips for your garden:

Single early tulips In most parts of the country, the single early tulips start to bloom the first two weeks of April. The flowers are available in a host of colors and bicolors, and many are pleasantly scented. Single early tulips are hardy and bloom on sturdy 10- to 12-inch stems. Plant bulbs 6 inches deep and 6 inches apart. Popular varieties include snow-white 'Diana,' the cardinal-red 'Couleur Cardinal,' and the spectacular salmon-and-red 'Princess Irene.'

Double early tulips The large, peonylike blossoms of the double early tulips are always welcome from early to mid-April. They are available in a variety of colors and bicolors and bloom on 8- to 10-inch stalks. Plant bulbs 8 inches deep and 6 inches apart. The rose-hued 'Peach Blossom' is a popular variety, or try any colorful mix sold in catalogs or through garden centers.

Unlike traditional tulips, which produce only one flower per stem, 'Georgette,' left, and other multiflowered varieties can produce a bouquet of three to seven blooms on every plant. Fringed tulips like 'Fancy Frills,' above, have extraordinary serrated petals. Plant both types of tulips along a garden path where you can enjoy them up close.

Mendel and triumph tulips Both mendel and triumph tulips are important to the bulb garden because they link the bloom seasons of the early flowering tulips with the late-flowering tulips. Blossoms usually appear in late April and early May. Mendel and triumph tulips come in a wide range of colors and bicolors and grow 18 to 24 inches tall. Bloom stalks are sturdy. Triumph tulips are hybrids of single early and late-flowering tulips. Plant bulbs 8 inches deep and 5 inches apart.

Darwin hybrid tulips For jumbo flowers and tall sturdy stems, you can't beat the darwin hybrids. The plants grow to 28 inches tall and produce larger flowers than any other tulip class. Darwin hybrids come in an assortment of brilliant colors and bicolors. Most bloom from late April to early May. Plant bulbs 8 inches deep and 6 inches apart. Popular varieties include yellow 'Sweet Harmony' and white 'Maureen.'

Lily-flowered tulips These graceful tulips add a touch of elegance to any garden with their unusual, pointed, slender blooms. The plants bloom in early May on 25-inch stems and are available in white, yellow, rose, red, and bicolored varieties. Plant 8 inches deep and 6 inches apart. Popular varieties include 'Aladdin,' the fiery-red 'Deep Shine,' and the pristine 'White Triumphator.'

Cottage tulips The cottage tulips, so named because they were first discovered growing in the small cottage gardens of Great Britain, often are the last tulips to bloom in the spring. The egg-shaped flowers are produced on 25- to 30-inch stems and come in many different colors and bicolors. Cottage tulips are particularly showy planted in mass. Plant bulbs 8 inches deep and 6 inches apart.

Rembrandt tulips The finely etched bicolored petals of the rembrandt tulips have made them longtime favorites with gardeners and artists alike. During the tulipomania period in Europe, the rembrandt tulips commanded the highest prices. Colors include red and yellow, red and cream, violet and yellow, and yellow and apricot. Rembrandt tulips make long-lasting and attractive cut flowers. The plants grow about 24 inches tall. Plant bulbs 8 inches deep and 6 inches apart.

Parrot tulips Brightly colored, ruffled petals give parrot tulips the exotic birdlike appearance that accounts for their name. They grow about 20 inches tall and sport a variety of vibrant colors and bicolors. The flower stalks are sturdy and withstand high winds. Parrot tulips are late bloomers that will grow in light shade. They also make ideal cut flowers. Plant bulbs 8 inches deep and 6 inches apart. Popular varieties include pinwheel red-and-white 'Estella Rijnveld' and apricot-pink 'Apricot Parrot.'

Mixing early blooming species tulips with other bulbs makes good sense if you want to double the color show in your garden. In this April garden, right, kaufmanniana tulip 'Johann Strauss' is the perfect partner for an underplanting of Scilla siberica. Both plants grow only 8 inches tall. Additional color is provided by the tulips' leaves, which have attractive maroon stripes.

Double late tulips The only real difference between the double late tulips and the double early tulips is the season of bloom. Double lates usually bloom in mid- to late May. They also grow a few inches taller than their early blooming cousins. Popular colors include rose, yellow, white, apricot, lavender, and bicolors. Plant bulbs 8 inches deep and 6 inches apart. Try the peonylike pink blooms of 'Angelique.'

Kaufmanniana tulips Kaufmanniana tulips often are the first tulips to bloom in the spring. Most varieties are bicolored with attractively mottled or striped foliage. The plants grow 6 inches tall and are a good choice for rock gardens. Kaufmanniana tulips look best when planted in mass. When fully open, kaufmanniana flowers resemble water lilies. Plant bulbs 8 inches deep and 6 inches apart. Try the elegant, pale salmon 'Fritz Keisler' in your garden.

Fosterana tulips The brightly colored, early flowering fosterana tulips have changed little since they were discovered growing wild on Turkish slopes 400 years ago. Most varieties grow 15 inches tall and bloom the same time as the kaufmanniana tulips. Use fosteriana tulips alone or in conjunction with other bulbs in midborder locations. Colors include white, salmon, yellow, and red, and many have variegated foliage. Fosterana tulips are extra hardy and long lived. Plant bulbs 8 inches deep and 6 inches apart.

Greigii tulips Beautifully marked foliage, large showy flowers, and sturdy, weather-resistant bloom stalks all make the greigii tulips an important addition to beds, borders, and rock gardens. The plants

planting and care

Before you plant tulips, be sure your planting bed is in good condition and receives full or partial sun. Till or spade the bed and rake the surface smooth. Then, dig a hole to the appropriate depth, place the bulb in the bottom of the hole, and cover the bulb with improved soil. To ensure success, add a little bonemeal to the bottom of each hole before planting the bulbs. Planting depths vary with each class of tulip. Tulips need cold weather to return year after year. In warmer climates, tulips are treated as annuals.

For an informal planting of tulips, gently scatter the bulbs over your garden bed and plant them where they fall. Use a trowel or bulb planter.

grow 10 inches tall and bloom from mid-April to early May. Colors include gold, crimson, yellow, salmon, red and white, yellow and red, and rose and white. The gray-green foliage often is striped with red, brown, or purple, making the greigii tulips a valuable border plant even after the flowers have faded. Plant bulbs 8 inches deep and 6 inches apart. Popular varieties include the reliable 'Red Riding Hood' and the red-and-white 'Plaisir.'

other species tulips

This class simply is a catchall for the many less commonly grown species tulips. All are wild tulips or hybrids. These tulips are hardy, colorful, and especially attractive in rock gardens. Bloom time varies from species to species; early species such as *T. pulchella* 'humilis' may bloom in February; other species such as acuminatea wait until May. Some of the most popular tulips in this category include tarda, chrysantha, turkestanica, whittallii, and eichleri.

Bonemeal or Holland bulb booster will help your plants grow stronger. Add some to the base of each hole and cover with a little soil before planting.

If you have just one or two dozen bulbs, dig a hole large enough for the entire group. Don't line them up in a row. Clumps of bulbs have more impact.

To keep rodents from eating your bulbs, plant the bulbs in a wire cage. The roots will grow through the wire, which keeps animals at bay.

anemone

Originally found blooming on hillsides in the Mediterranean and Central Asia, anemone, or windflower, sprouts forth with cheery daisylike blooms in a rainbow's selection of colors. An excellent naturalizer, anemone brightens any landscape in colors of purple, pink, red, and snow white in early spring. Although it grows only 4 to 6 inches tall, anemone produces carpets of bloom when planted in mass. Its green, fernlike foliage surrounds sweet blooms that close up at night and in inclement weather. In bloom for two to four weeks, anemone is a good choice for wooded locations and rock gardens.

selecting anemone for your garden

Here's a list of commonly available anemone for your garden:

A. apennina, Zones 6–9 The 2-inch-wide, daisylike white or light blue blooms of this anemone are borne on 6- to 9-inch stems. They bloom for almost a month and tolerate full sun to light shade.

A. blanda (Greek anemone), Zones 5–9 Blooming for two to four weeks, and eager naturalizers, *A. blanda* have larger flowers than *A. apennina*. Available in white, pink, and both light and dark blue, these self-sowing 6-inch beauties form a dense carpet of bloom. Their cheery, daisylike blooms do best in a well-drained planting site that receives partial shade.

planting and care

Anemone, like other spring-blooming bulbs, must be planted in autumn, although 'de caen' and 'St. Brigid' can be planted in the spring for summer flowers. Before planting, soak the small rhizomes in tepid water for 48 hours. Select a sunny planting spot or one that receives partial sun. The soil should be well drained; add sphagnum peat moss to help drainage. Place rhizomes in the ground 1 to 2 inches deep and leave 4 to 6 inches between them.

Rodents may find the tender anemone rhizomes delectable. Protect your plantings from invading mice and squirrels by layering chicken wire on top of the ground where the bulbs are planted.

chionodoxa

The Greeks called this bulb "glory-of-the-snow" because its stoic blooms sometimes push right up through the snow. The small, star-shaped blue blooms sparkle in rock gardens and borders and hold their brilliance for two to four weeks. Because they bloom early in spring, these bulbs can be planted under shrubs and trees and still reap the full sun exposure they need to be in top form. Left on their own, chionodoxa self-seeds and forms a dense carpet of bloom. Producing intense blue flowers, glory-of-the-snow is a popular choice for blue gardens that include blue muscari, anemone, crocus, and hyacinths.

selecting chionodoxa for your garden

Here's a list of commonly available chionodoxa for your garden:

C. luciliae, Zones 4–8 Growing 3 to 5 inches tall, these small wonders produce stalks of nodding blue blooms with a striking white eye. Six to 12 flowers per stalk are surrounded by attractive, grasslike foliage. Try the pink variety 'Pink Giant,' which produces 6-inch spires of pink flowers.

C. sardensis, Zones 4–8 A smaller, paler, and less floriferous version of *C. luciliae*, this chionodoxa produces stalks of light blue blooms with white centers.

planting and care

Once planted, chionodoxa requires no care. Although they need well-drained soil, no other special amendments are required. In early autumn, just place the small bulbs in the ground 3 inches deep and 3 inches apart in a spot that receives full sun. Each fall the plants will self-seed, so your initial investment will pay enormous dividends. Leave the plants undisturbed after they flower.

endymion

Commonly called wood hyacinths or Spanish blue-bells, these 8- to 10-inch-tall plants have spires of nodding, bell-shaped blooms. In pink, white, and blue, their pastel hues are beautiful intermixed or planted separately for drifts of the same color. Native to Spain and Portugal, they bloom in mid-spring and complement late-blooming varieties of tulips. Blooming in full sunlight or partial shade, wood hyacinths are excellent naturalizers. They are also sold under the names *Scilla campanulata* and *Scilla hispanica*.

selecting endymion for your garden

Wood hyacinths are excellent border and rock garden plantings. If you have the space, set wood hyacinths in your woodland garden. Their propensity to wander will produce glorious spreads of blooms.

planting and care

Select soil that is well drained in a sunny or partial shady spot. Plant bulbs 4 to 5 inches deep and allow 3 inches between each bulb.

Endymion hispanicus is easy to grow. Leave endymion alone once planted, and it will bloom for years.

eranthis

A member of the buttercup family, eranthis is Greek for "flower of spring." True to its name, this perky yellow flower is one of the earliest risers each spring. Commonly called winter aconite, this tiny plant produces sunny cup-shaped blooms that open to expose a crown of golden stamens. Blooming one to two weeks in the late winter to early spring, this little charmer easily self-sows.

selecting eranthis for your garden

E. hyemalis (Winter aconite), Zones 4–5
Growing 3 to 8 inches tall, the bright yellow blooms of winter aconite shine in the garden in the early spring. One of the first to bloom following winter, eranthis is an eager naturalizer.

planting and care

Eranthis requires no care once planted. Plant in the late summer or early fall, as soon as bulbs are available from your garden center. Once you've bought it, the sooner you plant it, the better, because it tends to dry out quickly, which inhibits bloom. To help things along, soak the bulbs in warm water for 24 hours, then plant 3 inches deep and 3 to 4 inches apart. Plant in sunny spots or underneath deciduous shrubs to allow full sun to bring out the best color in these little beauties. Once blooms are finished in the spring, allow the foliage to die back naturally.

Planting eranthis too late in the fall can keep the plant from blooming.

eremurus

The towering spires of eremurus, also called foxtail lily, appear in mid-spring. Although an underused bulb, eremurus makes a spectacular statement when planted in groups of four to six at the back of a border or bed. The name comes from the Greek words for solitary and tall, which describes perfectly the singular bloom clusters borne on plants that may grow 3 to 9 feet tall, depending on the variety. Available in a wide palette of colors, eremurus blooms in white, pink, yellow, orange, and peach. At home in any perennial border, eremurus is the first tall bloomer of the season and makes way for later tall perennials such as delphiniums and foxgloves. Blooms last about three weeks and are as beautiful in a border as they are in a bouquet.

selecting eremurus for your garden

Here's a list of commonly available eremurus for your garden:

E. robustus, Zones 4–5 As the variety name implies, this robust eremurus grows 8 to 9 feet tall, making it the tallest species of eremurus. Its light pink cluster blooms add early spring color to perennial borders and beds. Plant 4 inches deep with 12 inches between bulbs.

E. x 'Shelfordii,' Zones 4–5 These widely available hybrids also are the most colorful. Blooming in pastel shades of pink, yellow, orange, and peach, they are shorter than other varieties but still incredible back-of-the-border bloomers at 4 to 5 feet tall.

planting and care

In the fall select a place in your perennial bed that receives full sunlight. Place bulbs in rich soil, amended with sphagnum peat moss and compost or manure, 6 inches deep and 1 to 2 feet apart. Mulch with compost, especially in colder climates, to ensure hardiness.

In the early spring, remove the mulch after frost no longer is a danger or the shoots could be damaged from cold. After the blooms are gone in late spring, allow the foliage to wither and brown.

erythronium

Commonly called dog-tooth violets, erythronium is so named for its blossom, which is shaped like the tooth of a dog. Growing in clumps, the lily-shaped blooms have six petals with showy stamens and are surrounded by attractive dappled foliage. The slightly nodding blooms come in yellow, white, and lilac and hold their flowers for two weeks. Suited to growing in light shade, erythronium is at home in a woodland, as a landscape underplanting, or in a border.

selecting erythronium for your garden

Here's a list of commonly available erythronium for your garden:

E. americanum (Trout lily), Zones 4–5 Yellow blooms are borne on 1-foot-tall plants that are at home in a rock garden or woodland.

E. dens-canis (Dog-tooth violet), Zones 4–5 The 6- to 8-inch dog-tooth violets come in lilac, purple, and white. Flowering in the early spring, their foliage is mottled green with bronze markings.

E. revolutum, Zones 4–5 White blooms are borne on stems that reach 8 to 10 inches in height. Hybrids have produced striking yellow blooms. This plant does best when left alone.

E. x 'Pagoda,' Zones 3–9 Growing 10 to 12 inches tall, these mid-spring bloomers do best in moist soil and partial shade. Plant 4 inches deep, and leave 4 inches between bulbs.

planting and care

In the late summer or fall, plant corms 2 to 3 inches deep, spacing them 4 to 6 inches apart. Because erythronium does well in light shade, plant it in woodlands or in shaded areas under trees and shrubs. Soil should be well drained and amended with sphagnum peat moss and compost.

To propagate, dig up and remove small bulbs and replant in other areas. Erythronium is not bothered by pesky rodents—a benefit to gardens raided by rodents.

galanthus

Perhaps no other sight is more hope-inspiring than a solitary blooming clump of galanthus surrounded by a gray, lifeless woodland. The blooms of the commonly named snowdrop are among the first joyous signs that winter has lost its stronghold. The white, bell-shaped blossoms nod on short stalks. As persistent as it is delicate, the 3- to 8-inch snowdrop often pushes up through crusted snow and remains in bloom for two to four weeks.

selecting galanthus for your garden

Here's a list of commonly available galanthus for your garden:

G. elwesii (Giant snowdrop), Zones 4–5 These larger flowering snowdrops grow 6 to 8 inches tall. Blossoms are white with green inner markings. Plant giant snowdrop with smaller colorful bulbs that bloom at the same time, such as eranthis, scilla, and crocus.

G. nivalis (Common snowdrop), Zones 5–9 A smaller version of *G. elwesii*, common snowdrops grow 4 to 6 inches tall. Buy lots because they are inexpensive and often are sold in large quantities for naturalizing. 'Flore Pleno' is a double variety.

planting and care

In early fall, plant bulbs 2 to 4 inches deep, spacing them 2 to 3 inches apart. Snowdrops can be planted in full sun or in partial shade, which makes them excellent choices for woodlands and under trees and deciduous shrubs. Soil should be well drained and amended with sphagnum peat moss and compost. Many sources of galanthus are harvested from the wild, so be sure you buy your bulbs from reputable sources. Inexpensive and immune to rodent invasions, galanthus should be planted in large quantities to intensify its presence. Once planted, leave the plants alone and they will become more prolific with each passing year.

iris, Dutch

The exquisite and colorful blooms of the Dutch iris are cherished in the garden for their elegant presence. Coming into bloom in mid-spring, Dutch iris holds its blooms for one to two weeks. A myriad of blossom colors are available—from pure white and canary yellow to every shade in the spectrum of blue and purple. Exotic and hardy in the garden, Dutch iris also excels as cut flowers.

selecting Dutch iris for your garden

Dutch iris comes in a palette of wonderful shades and mixes. Dark velvety purple with yellow varieties are 'Purple Sensation,' 'Blue Ribbon,' and 'Romano.' For pastel versions of the same colors, try the light purple with yellow varieties such as 'Rosalie,' 'Silvery Beauty,' and 'Oriental Beauty.' A favorite all-yellow Dutch iris variety is 'Yellow Beauty.' For a lovely white iris with yellow touches, consider 'White Perfection.'

planting and care

In the autumn, select a spot that receives ample sun and plant bulbs 5 inches deep and 4 inches apart. Soil should be well drained. Once the blooms have faded, allow the spearlike foliage to die back naturally. If you're using the flowers for indoor bouquets, cut the blooms just as the buds begin to fatten. Dutch iris will not overwinter north of Zone 5. In colder regions, dig and store the bulbs like gladiolus.

ornithogalum

The starry white blooms of this European native are commonly called star-of-Bethlehem. Approximately 100 species of ornithogalum exist, many of which go by this common name. Plant height varies by species, and some grow as tall as 3 feet. The flowers, however, are similar, with six delicate petals fanned out to expose six stamens. Ornithogalum is a good choice for naturalizing because it is assertive and holds its lovely blooms for one to two weeks.

selecting ornithogalum for your garden

Here's a list of commonly available ornithogalum for your garden:

O. nutans, Zone 6 Blooming in the early spring, the hardy *O. nutans* produces single stems covered with 2-inch blooms. This variety does extremely well in partial shade and grows to 2 feet tall.

O. thyrsoides (Chincherinchee), Zone 8 The late-spring blooms of *O. thyrsoides*, commonly called chincherinchee or wonder flower, are delicate and star-shaped. Crowned atop a 6- to 18-inch-tall plant are 12 to 30 clustered blooms. Excellent as cut flowers, *O. thyrsoides* also are fragrant.

O. umbellatum (Star-of-Bethlehem), Zone 5 Excelling in both full sun or partial shade, *O. umbellatum* grows 8 to 12 inches tall and produces spikes of clustered blooms. Lovely star-shaped blossoms are as fragrant as they are delicate. Blooming in early spring, *O. umbellatum* bulbs and shoots have the added benefit of being impervious to rodents. They are good plants for rock gardens.

planting and care

A great choice for woodland gardens, ornithogalum naturalizes easily. In fact, bulbs multiply quickly and the plants self-sow readily. They may overpower a bed or border, so you may want to limit their territory to places where their vigorous nature will not be a problem.

Plant bulbs 3 to 4 inches deep and 2 to 3 inches apart. Although propagation is unnecessary, you can lift them following their bloom period and remove the small bulbs growing around the larger one. Replant the small bulbs immediately in another spot.

pushkinia

Although small in stature, pushkinia, commonly called striped squill, is one of the hardiest bulbs around. A member of the lily family and a cousin to chionodoxa, these early blooming bulbs produce 4- to 6-inch-tall spikes of loosely clustered blooms. The blooms are bluish-white, delicately penciled with a dark blue stripe running the length of each petal. Short and sweet, the fragrant pushkinia requires an attentive audience, so plant them where you can enjoy them—in front of a border or in a rock garden, for example.

selecting pushkinia for your garden

Here's a list of commonly available pushkinia for your garden:

P. scilloides, Zones 4–8 The small, bluish-white blooms with blue stripes measure ½ inch and are borne on 4- to 6-inch stalks. It is a good choice for rock gardens, naturalized in short grass, or as a front border planting along a path or sidewalk.

P. libanotica, Zones 4–8 This striped squill is virtually indistinguishable from *P. scilloides*.

planting and care

In the fall, plant pushkinia bulbs 3 inches deep and 3 inches apart in sandy soil. Select spots that receive either full sun or partial shade. These bulbs do best if left alone and will continue to bloom profusely if undisturbed, returning year after year with vigor. If blooming stops, dig up the bulbs and replant them in a different location. Because it self-seeds, pushkinia spreads generously. Often sold in large quantities for naturalizing, pushkinia blooms under deciduous trees and shrubs or tucked amid the grass in your lawn.

summer

Summer bulbs, sometimes called tender bulbs, combine the best characteristics of annual and perennial flowers. Like annuals, summer bulbs have a long season of bloom, and like perennials, they deliver year after year of service. In Northern gardens, summer bulbs must be dug up and stored each fall. In frost-free areas, summer bulbs can be left in the ground all year long. Holding their own among the showiest flowers, bulbs such as lilies, gladiolus, and dahlias offer a wide choice of colors and bloom shapes. Be sure to include some of the lesser-known summer bulbs in your garden, too. Plants—such as crinum, ixia, and eucomis—will add interest and color.

begonia (tuberous)

Electrify shady spots in your garden with tuberous begonias. These versatile beauties bloom in vibrant colors such as red, pink, yellow, orange, and white and in a wide assortment of flower forms. They are available in upright and trailing varieties, and give you the choice of double and single flowers. Choose upright varieties for pots, edgings, and borders, and use trailing types atop low walls and in hanging baskets. Best of all, tuberous begonias are perfect for containers, so you can place them where you need color the most and move them out of locations that receive constant, harsh sun. Although most tuberous begonias must be lifted in the fall and replanted in the spring, one species, *Begonia grandis*, tolerates moderately cold winters with a good layer of mulch.

selecting tuberous begonias for your garden

Here's a list of commonly available tuberous begonias for your garden:

B. grandis, Zones 6–10 If you are looking for a begonia that will survive the winter in the ground, try this species. Growing in a compact mound that reaches 1 to 2 feet tall, *B. grandis* produces flowers that are smaller than other types of begonias. Don't let that deter you, however. Subtly beautiful cascades of the petite light pink flowers nod gracefully from stunning red stems. Often called hardy begonia, it still needs a thick layer of mulch to protect the tubers over the winter. Hardy begonia does best in partially shady, moist locations.

B. x tuberhybrida, Zones 3–10 The most versatile, and certainly the showiest begonias, this group can be used in beds, window boxes, and containers. Blooming from early summer to the first frost, *B. tuberhybrida* hybrids produce an extraordinary assortment of colors and flower shapes. Here's a selection to keep in mind for all areas of your yard and garden.

To brighten a drab, shady porch, add a generous helping of potted 'Non-stop' begonias, right, teamed with shade-loving annuals coleus and impatiens. To keep the plants blooming, mix in a little liquid plant food every time you water. It's also smart to remove the flowers as they fade.

The bright colors of tuberous begonias make them ideal for the front of your flower border. Here, orange begonias contrast nicely with the silver gray foliage of cerastium, also called snow-in-summer.

Camellia type The elegant camellialike blooms of this begonia make it a popular choice. Double-flowering and lush, these varieties produce the largest flowers. Available in bold single colors such as hot pink, golden yellow, crisp white, and rich red, these double begonias also are available in the softest pastels. Bicolor varieties, such as the red-and-white 'Marmorata' are stunning. Growing 8 to 12 inches tall, camellia begonias bloom all summer. Lovely in beds, these upright plants also are excellent choices for containers. Plant several bulbs in each pot for the best effect.

Cascade type Popular for pots, hanging baskets, and window boxes, cascading tuberous begonias offer a waterfall of loose, luscious blossoms. The large pen-

Planted in an ornate terra-cotta pot, pink tuberous begonias add elegance to a low brick wall. Because containers, such as those opposite, dry out quickly, daily watering is a must. Keep the soil slightly moist at all times.

dulous blooms are available in a wide range of colors and look stunning dangling from a porch overhang or patio railing, or flowing out of containers on a deck. Growing 8 to 12 inches tall, these heavy-headed blooms are accented with lovely, intense green foliage. Plant them in a wind-protected location because their stiff stems break easily.

Carnation type Sometimes called fimbriata begonia, this variety has ruffled, fringed petals that mimic the carnation. Growing 8 to 12 inches tall, these upright plants look extraordinary in containers or planted among perennials in spots where they receive partial shade and are not exposed to the strong midday sun.

Picotee begonias These stunning begonias produce huge, ruffled bicolored flowers. Varieties include white, yellow, and orange flowers tipped with a startling penciled edge. Growing 8 to 12 inches tall, the lovely roselike flowers are good choices for containers and do best in partially shaded areas.

*'Non-stop Orange' bego-
nias, previous pages, live
up to their name by pro-
ducing wave after wave of
intensely colored flowers.
They're especially useful in
hanging baskets.*

*Just one plant of 'Bouton
de Rose,' left, is all you
need to add color and
excitement to a shade garden. Its striking translucent red blooms grow up to
6 inches in diameter.*

planting and care

To start tuberous begonias, buy hard, round tubers in April or May and place them in a low flat filled
with moist sphagnum peat moss. Be sure to set the tubers round side down. Place the flat in a bright
location, and when the begonias are about 3 inches tall, move them to soil-filled containers.

In the South, you can plant the tubers directly in the ground once the soil has warmed. Place tubers
in a hole 2 to 3 inches deep and cover them with soil. If you have started the plants from seeds or tubers
early, you can set the plants in the ground once the threat of frost has passed. A partially shady
location is best. Neither deep shade nor full sun is recommended. For striking color, plant three to five
tubers in the same location.

If planted in containers, tuberous begonias can dry out quickly; so make sure you keep them well
watered. Begonias in containers will tolerate sun, given enough moisture, but they do best in partial
shade. A well-balanced potting soil mixture high in sphagnum peat moss will help keep the plants
moist. If you want your begonias to bloom again next summer, dig up the tubers, remove the soil

'Non-stop' begonias A bit smaller than double begonias, these tiny titans make up in stamina what they lack in size. Their name is no marketing ploy, for these little compact begonias bloom nonstop nearly all summer. In fact, 'non-stop' begonias are so eager to bloom they'll often send up buds as soon as their first leaves appear. These hardy plants remain compact all summer, rarely growing over 12 inches tall. For this reason, they are particularly attractive planted in hanging baskets, planters, and window boxes. You also can tuck them into lackluster spots in your perennial border for instant and sustained color. Great in shady borders as a colorful edging plant, they are small and sturdy enough to be immune to wind damage. Just be sure to keep the plants well watered, and feed them often to help promote continuous flowering. For an outstanding color show, plant 'non-stop' begonias in groups of three or more. Although you can mix colors, you'll achieve more striking results if you mass plants of one color together. Or, blend two complementary shades in one pot or border. Good combinations include red and white, pink and yellow, and white and yellow. The most commonly available varieties of non-stop begonias are 'Orange,' 'Pink,' 'Yellow,' 'Red,' 'Copper,' and 'White.' If you have a sunny window or greenhouse, you also can grow 'non-stop' begonias indoors to brighten the dreary days of winter.

around them, and clip away the foliage before the first frost. Dry them for about two weeks in a warm, dry location. Store them in a box or sack filled with sphagnum peat moss or vermiculite until you replant in the spring.

Start tuberous begonias four to six weeks before the last expected frost. Plant the tubers round side down.

Grow in bright indirect light in a warm spot. Move the plants outdoors after the danger of frost has passed.

In summer, keep the soil evenly moist and mist the leaves on hot days. Feed them regularly with liquid plant food.

caladium

Caladium's heart-shaped and wildly colorful foliage puts most flowers to shame. Occasionally called angel-wings, this plant is more revered for its shapely and colorful leaves than for its insignificant flowers. Colorfully veined in vivid red, green, pink, white, and silver, its combinations and patterns make caladium look as if it is a painter's work in progress. Its jeweled tones shine when planted in containers on shaded terraces and patios. You also can plant them directly in the garden, or sink potted tubers into the ground. A native of the West Indies, caladium grows 8 to 20 inches tall.

selecting caladium for your garden

Here's a list of commonly available caladium for your garden:

C. bicolor, Zones 10–11 Growing wild in tropical rain forests, this caladium made an immediate hit with Victorian gardeners, who brought the exotic lovelies indoors. This species probably is the parent of *C. x hortulanum.*

C. x hortulanum (Fancy-leaved caladium), Zones 10–11 This rainbow-hued group has heart-shaped leaves splashed with red, pink, green, and white. Use in shaded, protected areas because too much sun fades their bright color and wind can rip their leaves. Plants grow 12 to 18 inches tall, and you may need to stake longer stems. Catalogs and garden centers carry many varieties. Some of the most com-

Caladium makes an excellent container plant. Here, a pair of large baskets packed with 'White Wing' caladium cheer up a dull entry.

monly available varieties include 'Frieda Hemple,' 'Fanny Munson,' 'Miss Chicago,' 'Pink Beauty,' 'Red Flash,' and 'Rosebud.' The popular white and green 'Candidum' is available in a dwarf version.

In this shady, out-of-the-way garden corner, left, a colorful mixture of caladiums is protected from high winds and hot sun by a low brick wall.

planting and care

Start caladium indoors four to six weeks before the last expected frost. Using a flat filled with potting soil, place the tubers round side up 1 inch apart. Cover lightly with a mixture of half peat and half perlite; water generously, and place in a warm, bright location. When the plants are several inches tall, transplant the young caladium to 4-inch pots.

When the outside temperature no longer drops below 60° F, plant small caladium in well-drained soil 2 to 3 inches deep, leaving 3 to 4 inches between each plant. Caladium does best grown in a shaded, well-protected area. Although a little sunlight gives them a more intense color, too much sunlight fades them. To encourage leaf production, remove the small flowers as they are produced. Water frequently, and mist the foliage on hot days.

When the leaves die back in the fall, dig the tubers. Allow them to dry for several days, then remove the excess soil and foliage. Store the tubers in dry sand, sphagnum peat moss, or vermiculite in a cool, dry frost-free area. Replant the bulbs in the spring.

Add color under trees by sinking pots of caladium in the ground. When the plants go dormant, dig up the pots.

89

canna lily

The canna lily's torchlike blooms and large sculpted leaves are a common sight in parks and estate gardens. You don't need a huge garden, however, to make use of this grand plant. If you want all-summer color with a little tropical spice, canna lilies are ideal. Both the 6-foot-tall standard canna and the dwarf canna, which grows only 3 feet tall, are available in varieties that bloom in apricot, orange, red, white, pink, and yellow. Foliage may be bright green or red-bronze, depending on the variety. Plant dwarf cannas in beds of their own, or mix them with annual flowers. Use standard cannas in back-of-the-border locations, or try them as temporary screens.

selecting canna lilies for your garden

Here's a list of commonly available canna lilies for your garden:

C. x generalis (Common garden canna), Zones 3–11
Available in standard and dwarf varieties, canna hybrids offer a variety of heights and colors to choose from. Most attractive when planted in groups, cannas bloom all summer, never missing a beat until frost.

Standard cannas Growing from 3 to 6 feet tall, these hybrids sometimes are referred to as giant cannas because of their great height. In the back of the border or as a screen or temporary hedge, cannas fill in space with great flourish. Requiring a sunny spot and lots of moisture, cannas thrive in

'Tropical Rose' canna, right, is the first canna lily developed that you can grow from seed. Sow the seeds indoors 8 to 10 weeks before the last expected frost, and move the seedlings outdoors when the weather warms.

extreme heat. Popular varieties include 'The President,' which produces a striking all-red flower, 'Yellow King Humbert,' which is golden yellow with a red-splashed throat, or the showy orange 'Wyoming,' which has purple-tinted leaves.

Dwarf cannas Pared down to a bushy 2 to 3 feet tall, dwarf cannas are excellent choices for beds as well as for planters and containers. Blooming all summer, dwarf cannas are available in a wide choice of colors.

'Pfitzer's' series dwarf varieties include the 'Crimson Beauty,' 'Chinese Coral,' 'Primrose Yellow,' and 'Salmon Pink.'

One new variety, 'Tropical Rose,' is the only dwarf canna lily you can grow from seed. Producing exquisite pink blooms, 'Tropical Rose' is a great addition to annual flower gardens because it grows only 2 feet tall. Start the seeds in a sunny window or greenhouse in the late winter. To prevent transplant shock, sow the seeds in peat pots which you can plant directly into the garden without disturbing the plant roots. When the danger of frost has passed, move the canna seedlings outdoors, spacing the plants about 18 inches apart. In the North, dig up the rhizomes in the fall and store as you would with other cannas.

Tall, standard-sized cannas make excellent temporary screens or windbreaks. In this narrow side yard, left, 'The President' canna grows behind a mass planting of bright pink cleome. Both species grow quickly and produce lots of color with little care.

planting and care

Start canna lilies inside one month before the last frost in the spring, or plant them outdoors after the danger of frost has passed. Place each rhizome horizontally in the ground and cover with an inch or two of soil. Cannas like rich, moist soil and should be fed several times during the growing season with a balanced liquid fertilizer.

In the South, canna lilies may be left in the ground all year; in the North, the rhizomes should be lifted after the plants have been blackened by frost. Dig the rhizomes, clip off the withered foliage, and store in dry sand or vermiculite in a frost-free location. To propagate, divide the rhizomes in early spring before planting.

dahlia

Dahlias are tireless performers in any garden drama. Native to Mexico, where they grow wild on hillsides, these tender bulbs bloom in many colors from summer till frost. Dahlias vary in height, too, so you're likely to find one to star in your garden production.

Dahlias vary so much in form and size that they are divided into classes, each of which offers a full range of colors, heights, and bloom types. The class list includes single, anemone, decorative, cactus, semicactus, ball, and pompon, as well as many other descriptive names commonly used by nurseries. Plant height is perhaps the most important consideration when you select dahlias for your

The brilliant orange-yellow blooms of 'Chinese Lantern,' below, are so bright they almost seem to glow in the dark. 'Sisa,' right, produces bouquets of sunny yellow flowers from midsummer till frost. Both varieties grow about 3 feet tall. Since these are tender, they require much care for overwintering.

'Pryts Glorie' is just one of the many dahlias you can grow that have bicolored blooms. Its large rounded flowers look as if they've been carefully dipped in purple paint. The blooms of 'Pryts Glorie' also make wonderful cut flowers.

Single-flowered dahlia varieties generally are a little shorter than their showier cousins. 'Sneezy,' above, grows 2 feet tall and develops masses of snow-white flowers that last for days in a cut flower arrangement. 'Victory Dwarf Orange,' right, is even smaller, reaching only 12 to 18 inches tall.

garden. Because they range in height from 1 to 7 feet, dahlias have considerable landscaping possibilities. And because they produce 15 to 40 flowers per plant, you get a lot of bloom from just several plants grouped together. Tall types belong at the back of the border, while medium-size varieties look best massed together or combined with other flowers in the middle of a garden. Dwarf dahlias can be planted along the edges of borders or potted for patio display.

In Southern climates, dahlias are hardy and can remain in the ground over winter. In the North, you must dig the tender tubers and store them until spring. The little time this takes is well worth the effort, because they are so versatile in gardening situations and make wonder-

An inner circle of smaller petals gives 'Alstergrusz' its unique appearance. This eye-catching but unusual form goes by different names. Some nurseries classify it as a collarette; others call it an anemone-flowered dahlia. Still others refer to it as a butterfly dahlia. By whatever name, it's spectacular.

If you didn't know better, you could easily mistake the graceful flowers of 'Berliner Kleene' dahlia for those of a tropical water lily. Growing to 3 feet tall, 'Berliner Kleene' may require staking in windy locations. Always insert the stake at planting time and tie the plant to it as growth appears. Don't jam the stake into the ground after the dahlia has already reached maturity. You might puncture the tubers.

planting and care

Planting dahlias early indoors will give you a head start on summer flowering. About six weeks before the last expected frost in your area, plant each tuber in a 5-inch pot filled with an all-purpose potting mix. Place the pots on a sunny windowsill and keep the medium moist. Outdoor planting can begin as soon as all threat of frost is past. Dahlias perform best in a sunny location in rich, well-drained soil. Mature height dictates planting depth and spacing. Set tubers of tall types (reaching more than 2½ feet tall) 3 to 4 inches deep and 20 inches apart. Plant shorter varieties 2 to 3 inches deep and 10 inches apart.

After frost has blackened dahlia foliage, carefully dig up the tubers with a spading fork. Gently shake away any clinging soil and pull off shriveled or rotting tubers.

ful, long-lasting bouquets. In the garden they provide all-summer bloom, and each blossom holds its brilliance for two weeks.

selecting dahlias for your garden

Dahlias grow in Zones 3–11. Here's a list of commonly available dahlias for your garden:

Single Also called mignon dahlias, these short, stocky dahlias grow 16 to 20 inches tall and have single flowers 3 to 4 inches wide.

Anemone Anemone look-alikes, these dahlias grow about 18 inches tall and sport semidouble flowers 2 to 3 inches across.

Decorative The most common dahlia form, decorative dahlias have open, rounded blooms and come in a wide range of sizes. The tallest varieties often are called dinner-plate dahlias because of their bloom size.

Cactus and Semicactus As their name suggests, these dahlias have the starburst shape of a cactus flower. They come in a wide range of brilliant colors and sizes.

Ball Though other dahlias seem to relax, the 4- to 5-inch, ball-shaped dahlias stand up straight and display a perky attitude. These vigorous dahlias grow 3 to 4 feet tall.

Pompon Even more tightly formed than the ball-shaped dahlias, the petals of pompon dahlias are compact. Their upright blooms, 2 to 3 inches across, are borne on long stems, making them excellent for cutting. In a barrage of bright and pastel colors, pompon dahlias grow 2 to 3 feet tall.

Use pruning shears to clip away the dead and dying foliage. Be sure to leave 2 to 3 inches of stem attached to the tubers. Now is a good time to label each variety.

Wash all remaining soil from the tubers with your garden hose. You may have to carefully spread the tubers apart to remove the soil wedged between them.

While the tubers are still slightly damp, plunge them into a box filled with dry vermiculite. Cover the tubers completely and top with a layer of newspapers. Store in a cool, dry location.

gladiolus

Plant gladiolus and you'll soon know why it's cherished by gardening beginners and experts alike. Native to South Africa, the gladiolus has been a favorite in this country for years. Old names for gladiolus include sword lily, which refers to its sword-shaped leaves. Blooming in nearly every color of the rainbow, gladiolus is especially eye-catching planted along a fence or wall. These plants vary in size and are divided into classes, from miniatures to giants. They are so simple to grow and so beautiful to behold that no garden or yard should be without them.

Unrivaled as a cut flower, the gladiolus blooms from the bottom to the top, filling the entire stalk with extravagantly rippled flowers. They'll hold their bloom for about a week; to prolong the vase life, cut the stems as the lower flowers fade.

Gladiolus flowers appear two to three months after you plant the corms. The bulbs are inexpensive and widely available from garden centers and catalogs. For color all summer, plant a new crop every two weeks from late spring until midsummer. In the South, the gladiolus can remain in the ground over the winter. In areas where temperatures dip below freezing, you must dig the corms and store them in a cool place until spring.

selecting gladiolus for your garden

Here's a list of commonly available gladiolus bulbs for your garden:

Gladiolus hybrid standard varieties, Zones 3–11 Hybridizers have been successful in creating a wide range of solid and bicolor flower combinations. Regardless of the color, the plant's tall, elegant flower stalks are extraordinary in bouquets by themselves or mixed with other flowers.

'Big Time Supreme' gladiolus, right, lives up to its name by producing tall spikes of extra-large, candy-pink flowers. In rich soil, standard gladiolus varieties such as 'Big Time Supreme' can grow up to 6 feet tall. Stake them to prevent shearing during windstorms.

Rich, deep purple flowers are the calling card of the 'Passion' gladiolus, left. A standard variety, 'Passion' may grow to 5 feet tall. Like other bulbs, gladiolus look their best when planted in groups or clumps scattered throughout the garden. In the flower border above, the plants make a big impression.

Growing 3 to 4 feet tall, the lightly ruffled buds cover most of the stem, opening in slow succession, from bottom to top.

Gladiolus hybrid miniature varieties, Zones 3–11

Miniature gladiolus, called 'Tiny-Tot' or 'Butterfly' gladiolus, produces 2- to 3-foot-tall flower stalks. Its blooms are smaller than those of the standard gladiolus, but the wide array of color choices is the same. The compact growth of miniature gladiolus makes it unequaled for cut flowers and arrangements. You also can plant

Standard gladiolus, such as this lovely cluster of pink 'Orleans,' probably is the easiest cut flower you can grow. To enjoy bouquets of your favorite varieties all summer, plant corms wherever you have any open space in your garden. Vegetable gardens are an ideal location—as you harvest early spring crops, replace them with gladiolus.

twice as many in the same space as standard-sized varieties. They require no staking to keep them upright in heavy weather.

G. nanus, Zones 3–10 This miniature version of the statuesque gladiolus is excellent in borders and in rows to harvest as cut flowers. Growing 1½ to 2 feet tall, these small gladiolus should be planted 4 inches deep and 3 inches from other corms. Blooming in July and August, they are available in red, white, pink, and rose. Unlike standard gladiolus varieties, *G. nanus* will overwinter in the garden through Zone 5. In the northern part of its range, be sure to cover plants with several inches of mulch to help the plants survive winter.

Many gladiolus va____ ____iant bicolored flowers. For example, the flowers of 'Sara Jane,' left, are pink-peach petals with darke___ ____ ____ ____ y display a complementary color in the form of stripes, spots, or blotches. These varieties all look ____ ____ ____ ___ r in a vase by themselves. Bicolors come in a wide range of flower shades.

n bed. Plant jumbo corms 6 inches deep; medium-sized
eep. Leave about 5 inches between each corm. Cover
best effect, plant gladiolus in rows or clumps of four,
tall varieties, mound soil around plant bases. As the
event plants from falling over.

in simple rows so you can harvest them effortlessly.
oms all summer long. To liven up a waning summer
adiolus corms.
ezing, gladiolus
ou must dig up
llow the foliage
om the ground
rom the corms
ottoms of the
lace. Store the

To produce a constant supply of cut flowers, plant new crops of corms every two weeks. Remember, big corms give big blooms.

PriL
liPs
lostas · points poke-through ground
inmental Rhubarb - first leaf Red
rocynthia · buds green
(leaf)
ome Roses · buds - Red
ilacs - leaf buds Red/purple
isteria · bud, leaves
imbing
utorn Grasses
Queen of the Prairie Leaves
Apple Tree leaves
rocynthia Yellow blossoms

lily

The dazzling trumpetlike blooms of the lily are the backbone of any summer garden. These hardy bloomers will provide your garden with exciting color and fragrance, and give a bountiful harvest of blooms for cutting. Easy to grow, lilies are favorites of northern gardeners because they overwinter in the ground. If well mulched, most lilies will return year after year with their stately and extravagant blossoms. Lilies are a strong element in mixed borders. Growing 2 to 6 feet tall, these versatile plants most often are used to add dependable backup color behind shorter flowers. Planted in late summer or early autumn, these delightful all-time favorites will perform in all their glory the following summer.

To enhance the natural drama of lilies, consider planting one variety en masse. Undulating waves of color are a striking effect you can achieve easily. The welcoming trumpet shape of the lily makes it an excellent dooryard garden companion or a walkway edging. For best results, plant three or more bulbs of each variety you choose. If mixing varieties, put taller ones in back.

Lilies grown in containers are both beautiful and portable. For your own movable feast of color, try

shorter varieties such as the 18-inch 'Connecticut Lemon Glow.' Purchase bulbs in the spring and plant them 4 inches deep. An 8- or 10-inch pot will hold three bulbs. For best performance the following season, transplant bulbs into the garden after all the foliage has died back.

selecting lilies for your garden

Here's a list of commonly available lilies for your garden:

Asiatic hybrid lilies, Zones 3–8 Asiatic hybrids perform the opening act in early summer. In both perennial beds and bouquets, the lovely reflexed blooms of Asiatic lilies are star performers. Prolific bloomers, each stem can bear up to 12 flowers. June bloomers include the 15- to 20-inch-tall 'Orange Flame,' the popular orange-red 'Enchantment,' which grows to 4 feet tall, and the 3-foot-tall lemon-hued 'Connecticut King.'

One of the best known Asiatic hybrid lilies, 'Connecticut King,' above, bursts forth in midsummer with shimmering yellow flowers. 'Make-Up,' opposite, another Asiatic, has coral-peach blooms that seem to change color as the sun passes overhead. It also blooms in midsummer. Both grow about 3 feet tall.

Spectacular! That's the only way to describe the bright orange blooms of 'Pasa Dena.' An Asiatic hybrid lily, 'Pasa Dena' performs in June and July, growing about 3 feet tall. Plant six to 12 bulbs together in the center of your perennial border or in a bed by themselves. They look particularly good planted near yellow flowers such as coreopsis or rudbeckia.

Aurelian lily (Trumpet lily), Zones 3–8 Also called trumpet lilies, Aurelian hybrids blossom in midsummer and continue on through August. Fragrant and tall, growing 4 to 5 feet, trumpet lilies are excellent back-of-the-border choices. Easy to grow, and willing to return year after year, Aurelian lilies require little care. Standouts in this cast include the 4-foot-tall white 'Regale,' which has striking bright orange anthers, and the 4- to 5-foot-tall 'Golden Splendor,' a cheery yellow flowering lily that produces as many as 20 flowers per stem.

L. lancifolium (Tiger lily), Zones 3–8 No old-fashioned garden would be complete without the speckled blooms of the tiger lily.

Asiatic and Oriental lilies, left, are an unbeatable combination, especially when plant-ed in a border with summer perennials like bee balm, daylily, coneflower, Russian sage, artemisia, and aster. 'Côte d'Azur,' above, is another Asiatic hybrid lily that displays its flowers in June and July. Its rich, reddish-purple blooms are lovely to look at in the garden or as a cut flower.

Thanks to cultivation, the standard orange tiger lily is joined by a wide array of additional colors, including white, yellow, pink, and red. Flowering from July to September, tiger lilies produce bountiful blooms, up to 20 flowers per stem. Excellent for beds and borders, hybrid tiger lilies grow 2 to 4 feet tall. These hardy lilies also are 2 to 3 inches across, good choices for naturalizing.

Turk's-cap lilies, Zones 3–8 Many lily species go by the common name Turk's-cap. The reflexed petals in an elegant upswing, much like a turban, are what gives this exotic, stunning lily its common name. *L. henryi* is a tall, old-fashioned favorite with as many as 20 orange flowers per stem. The glossy red blooms of *L. chalcedonicum* nod atop upright stalks and bloom in early summer. The dark

Madonna lilies, Lilium candidum, above, have fragrant, snow-white blooms in early summer. Unlike other lilies, Madonna needs to be planted just under the surface of the soil. Its bloom stalks are 3 feet tall. 'Enchantment' lily, right, is probably the best known Asiatic hybrid lily. A garden standard for years, 'Enchantment' is a reliable perennial, growing bigger and better every year. In rich soil and a sunny location, 'Enchantment' may grow 4 feet tall. The bright orange blooms appear in midsummer.

The tall, nodding bloom stalks of Turk's-cap lily appear in early summer. It is one of the best species for partially shady, woodland settings. Although Turk's-cap lilies can grow 6 feet tall, they don't need staking.

rose, spotted flowers of *L. martagon* do best in partially shaded areas. Growing 5 to 6 feet tall, this Turk's-cap lily also has an all-white variety, 'Album.' *L. pyrenaicum*, also known as yellow Turk's-cap, is a hardy, early bloomer with yellow flowers. Also available are a number of Turk's-cap hybrids that sport the lovely, nodding bloom shapes of species Turk's-cap lilies.

L. candidum (Madonna lily), Zones 3–8 The image of this dazzling lily speaks of purity and goodness. Add antiquity to that list, because the regal Madonna lily has been in cultivation for nearly 3,500 years.

planting and care

Most lilies require a sunny location, although some, like Turk's-cap, prefer a partially shaded spot. Prepare the bed by digging a hole and adding well-rotted manure or other organic material. If the site is too wet, add sand. Lilies excel in raised beds, where excess water can drain away from their roots. Add a well-balanced fertilizer or bonemeal to the bed before you set in the bulbs.

Large lilies require lots of room, so allow at least 1 foot between each bulb. Lilies produce the best show if they are grouped, so plant at least three bulbs together in a triangle, leaving about 8 to 12 inches between each bulb. Smaller lilies can be planted 4 to 6 inches apart. If you plant the bulbs in an area where you'll be planting other flowers or bulbs, mark the position of the lilies with a stake. Before filling the hole, mix in a well-balanced fertilizer and additional organic materials to the cover soil, then fill the area, lightly tamping down the soil. Lilies benefit from mulch, so add a thick layer of straw or leaves on top for the winter.

In the spring, when the shoots have broken ground, add additional mulch to protect lilies from late-season frosts. As the plants grow, you

Dig a hole for each bulb; make the hole big enough for the roots to spread. Gently untangle the roots before you set the bulb in place.

Its large, trumpet-shaped white blossoms are accented with yellow anthers. Known for a rich fragrance, these lovely flowers are borne on 3- to 4-foot-tall stems. Plant bulbs as soon as you receive them (usually in the early autumn).

L. speciosum (Japanese lily), Zones 5–11 Growing 4 to 5 feet tall, this popular lily is a favorite of florists and gardeners alike. The variety 'Rubrum' is a glorious rose-hued flower, edged with white and spotted with darker rose along the length of the petal. 'Album,' an old-fashioned white variety, grows to 5 feet tall.

L. longiflorum (Easter lily), Zones 7–9 This classic lily, a popular potted plant in late spring, also can grow in the garden in warmer climates. Its snow white blooms with showy yellow-orange anthers contrast nicely with glossy, deep green leaves. Easter lilies grow 16 to 18 inches tall on sturdy stems.

Oriental lilies For information about Oriental lilies, see pages 148–153.

may want to stake the taller varieties. The first lilies start blooming in midsummer; keep lilies in top shape by removing the flowers as soon as they fade.

In late summer to fall, the leaves will start to yellow. When the foliage has completely withered, cut it back to ground level and mulch heavily. If you want to lift and separate lilies, fall is the time to do this. Otherwise, most species can be left in place.

Sprinkle a handful of bonemeal in the bottom of each hole. Plant lilies in clumps of at least three bulbs of the same type and color.

Support taller varieties with stakes. Position the stakes at planting time to help you remember next spring where the bulbs are planted.

Gently tamp the soil down to eliminate air pockets. In Northern climates, mulch planting areas with straw or leaves for winter protection.

zantedeschia

The wet marshy areas of South Africa are the home of zantedeschia, the calla lily, where its ubiquitous appearance has earned it the name ditch lily. Everywhere else in the world, however, the elegant calla lily is held in high regard. From the Greek word meaning 'beautiful,' the lovely calla lives up to its name. The shapely spathes are rich and velvety, looking more artifice than flower.

Loving moist, nearly swampy places, the larger callas are good border plants for water gardens and will grow even in shallow standing water. Smaller calla species grow well in borders, beds, and containers. In areas free of killing frosts, callas will stay green all winter. Known primarily as a greenhouse or indoor plant, the calla lily deserves more recognition as a tender outdoor bloomer, happy in full sun or light shade. Mature plants grow 24 inches tall and are available in white, yellow, pink, cream, and apricot varieties. All varieties have mottled foliage.

selecting zantedeschia for your garden

Here's a list of commonly available zantedeschia for your garden:

Z. aethiopica (Calla lily, arum lily), Zones 9–11 Loving full sun, this species also likes moist, boggy soil and excels in water gardens. In winter, except in the warmest of climates, bring the bulbs indoors. Even in warm areas, mulch over the top of the plant to guard it from occasional light frosts. 'Green Goddess,' a green-spathed variety is a good choice. Use Z. *aethiopica* in pots and planters that you can move around to gain color where you need it the most. Grown this way, zantedeschia are easy to harvest and store during the winter months. This species of calla is now available in a wide range of pastel colors. When the plants are finished blooming, remove the dead blooms and enjoy the plant's extraordinary mottled foliage.

Z. elliottiana, Zones 9–11 This bright gold-flowered calla grows 15 to 18 inches tall and is an excellent choice for beds and borders. Plant it in a container so you can enjoy its buttery blooms all summer long, then move it indoors before the first frost. Its stately and patrician presence made this golden calla a favorite Victorian parlor plant.

Z. rehmannii, Zones 9–11 A showy calla, it has delicate pink flowers deepening to rose at the edges. Growing 15 to 18 inches tall, this calla is extraordinary blooming outside as well as inside. Incredibly

Originally available only in white, calla lilies, opposite, now come in yellow, pink, salmon, lavender, peach, apricot, and cream. All varieties have bright green leaves mottled with white spots.

long lasting when cut, a few callas in an upright vase make an elegant centerpiece. Variety 'Dwarf Pink' grows just 12 inches tall with flowers that measure 2 to 3 inches in diameter. Try it in pots or planters mixed with low-growing annuals.

'Giant White' calla lilies, left, can grow to 3 feet tall with showy, pure-white flowers. The blooms, which can measure 8 inches across, make long-lasting cut flowers.

planting and care

Start calla lilies indoors in March or April to fill the garden with delicate flowers by May and June. Or, plant directly outdoors when the soil warms up. Space rhizomes about 12 inches apart in the garden and cover with about 3 inches of soil at planting time. For best growth, calla lilies need rich organic soil, lots of water, and liquid feeding every two or three weeks. Callas will survive mild winters where it frosts occasionally.

If you live in a hot, dry climate, try callas in containers because they thrive best in moist, rich soil. Pot them up and place them on shaded patios or porches. Containers dry out quickly, so be sure to monitor soil moisture on a regular basis. Planting callas in containers makes it easier to move callas indoors in colder climates.

In the North, dig the rhizomes after frost has darkened the foliage and store them dry in sand or vermiculite. In the South, you can leave them in the garden all year long. If you want to grow calla lilies indoors, as was popular in the 19th century, you should start calla lilies every four to six weeks in a greenhouse to ensure continuous bloom.

acidanthera

If you believe in saving the best for last, you'll appreciate the classic, nodding blooms of acidanthera. Its appearance in the garden in late summer is a joyful sight amid the waning perennials. This fragrant and elegant flower is grossly underused in summer gardens. A native of the tropics, acidanthera grows 1 to 2 feet tall. In beds and borders or in pots and containers, these flowers are an exotic addition to any location. Acidanthera's common name, peacock orchid, hints of its showy presence in the garden. A favorite cut flower, acidanthera is revered for its subtle beauty and for its lovely fragrance.

selecting acidanthera for your garden

A. bicolor, Zones 3–11 Although sometimes sold as abyssinian gladiolus, *A. bicolor* is the true name of this species. Surrounded by sword-shaped leaves, the 2-foot-tall stems are topped with creamy white flowers that have six petals and are marked with burgundy at the base. Lovely in cut-flower arrangements, they are sweetly scented, too.

planting and care

In the spring, after the danger of frost has passed, plant the corms in a sunny, well-drained location. Dig a hole 3 to 4 inches deep, and allow 4 to 6 inches between corms. Cover them with soil and water.

Acidanthera also shines as a container plant. To grow them in pots, start the corms early indoors. Then move them outdoors as soon as the danger of frost is over. When the corms are planted directly in the ground, they produce flowers in late summer.

If you live in the South, you can leave the corms in the ground over the winter. In the North, lift the corms before the first frost, and store them like gladiolus.

agapanthus

Waving its loose, globular lilac-hued blossoms in the wind, agapanthus could be mistaken for an allium. A native of South Africa, agapanthus often is called by its geographically incorrect name, lily-of-the-Nile. Regardless of its upbringing, the lovely lavender star-shaped blooms of agapanthus, borne on 2-foot-tall stems, makes them showy newcomers to any garden. Because it is so tender, agapanthus is a good candidate for container gardening. Its lovely straplike leaves all but cover the tops of most containers, and the plants look stunning on patios and terraces where they enjoy a variety of conditions, from full sun to partial shade. In winter, bring the plants indoors, where they'll continue to bloom if placed in south-facing windows.

selecting agapanthus for your garden

Here's a list of commonly available agapanthus for your garden:

A. africanus (African lily, lily-of-the-Nile), Zones 9–11 Available in light blue and white, this agapanthus species grows 12 to 18 inches tall and bears clusters of 1- to 4- inch blossoms. The leaves are clumplike at the base of the plant.

A. orientalis, Zones 9–11 Growing 2 to 3 feet tall, this agapanthus has 2-inch-wide purple-blue flowers that do best growing in full sun.

planting and care

Intolerant of frost, this temperature-sensitive beauty should be moved indoors before the weather turns cold. Therefore, it's best to plant agapanthus in containers. To include them in your garden borders, simply sink the plant, pot and all, into a hole. Then, when cold weather threatens, quickly dig up your plants and whisk them to the warmth of indoors. Keep the plants near a sunny window or in a greenhouse until the danger of frost disappears in the spring.

amaryllis

You probably think of amaryllis as the generous, trumpet-shaped beauties you can force indoors. In the summer, however, these popular Dutch hybrids can be grown outdoors in containers or in the garden. One species, *Amaryllis belladonna*, produces bare stalks topped with translucent pink flowers. Because their blooms are borne on tall, leafless stems, they earned the risque name naked lady. Its more familiar name, belladonna lily, means beautiful lady. Regardless of the zone, you can have amaryllis in the garden for the summer. In colder climates, plant them in containers if you want to bring them indoors when the temperature drops.

selecting amaryllis for your garden

Here's a list of commonly available amaryllis for your garden:

Dutch hybrid amaryllis (Hippeastrum), Zones 9–11 This is truly a plant for all seasons. Forced indoors, it blooms all winter, then when the weather warms, you can move it outdoors for the summer. In the South, amaryllis can stay in the garden year-round. For colder climates, allow amaryllis to summer outdoors, then move it inside for the cold weather. See pages 162–167 for information about varieties.

A. belladonna (Belladonna lily), Zones 9–11 This beautiful plant has pink or white lilylike blooms borne on bare 18-inch-tall stalks. The fragrant flowers open to 3 to 4 inches wide. Blooming in late summer, belladonna lily requires a protected spot so its long stems will not be damaged by wind.

planting and care

In the spring when the weather is reliably warm, move potted amaryllis outdoors to a spot protected from strong sunlight. Wait until the threat of frost has safely passed and tuck the bulbs, or the entire pot, into a bed or border. In hot climates, amaryllis can be planted outdoors year-round. Once the flowers have faded, cut the stem back to 2 inches. In the fall when the foliage has yellowed, lift the bulbs and store them indoors at a temperature of 48 to 55 degrees Fahrenheit. When repotting, you can pull off the offsets at the side of the bulb and plant these in separate containers.

anemone

Anemone is called windflower because it seems to grow as spontaneously as if it were sown by the wind. Two summer-blooming varieties make colorful border additions as well as great cut flowers. The 'de caen' varieties are single flowered, and the 'St. Brigid' varieties are double petaled. Flowering July through August, their cheery daisylike blooms are available in purple, pink, red, blue, and white, with bold markings. They hold their joyous bloom for two weeks.

selecting anemone for your garden

A. coronaria 'de caen' and 'St. Brigid,' Zones 5–8 Native to the Holy Land, and hardy in warmer climates, the poppy-flowered anemone produces marvelous color when grouped together in a perennial border. The flowers are 1½ to 2½ inches wide and are borne on 12- to 14-inch stems. Blooming in partial shade as well as in a sunny, sheltered site, the single 'de caen' anemone and the double 'St. Brigid' anemone are excellent cutting flowers.

planting and care

Plant in spring or fall. Before planting, soak the small rhizomes in tepid water for 48 hours. Select a sunny or partly sunny planting spot. The soil should be well drained; add sphagnum peat moss to help drainage. Place the rhizomes in the ground 1 to 2 inches deep and leave 4 to 6 inches between bulbs.

After blooms have faded, allow the foliage to die before clipping. If the blooms begin to diminish after several years, lift and divide the tubers. Dry for a few days, then replant in another area. In colder climates, *A. coronaria* is not hardy and is best treated as an annual.

crinum

The elegant, trumpet-shaped flowers of crinum bring an air of the tropics to the garden. The blooms are lilylike in appearance, so much so that the Greek name for lily is crinum. In fact, however, crinum is a member of the amaryllis family. There are 130 species of crinum, and nearly all are tropical, so they make ideal choices for southern gardens. Although they are intolerant of frost and require heavy mulching even in southern gardens, they are easy to grow in containers, which you can move when the weather turns cold.

selecting crinum for your garden

Here's a list of commonly available crinum for your garden:

C. bulbispermum, Zones 8–11 With a layer of mulch in the fall to protect the tender bulbs, you can expect this species to return in areas no colder than Zone 8. Reaching 3 feet tall, this native of South Africa grows in partial shade and produces 4-inch white blooms with rich red veins.

C. x powellii, Zones 8–11 Although this hybrid, related to *C. bulbispermum*, will tolerate light frost, you need to lift the bulbs in areas that receive sustained cold weather. In southern gardens, you can try to overwinter your crinum by applying a thick layer of mulch. The trumpet-shaped blooms are available in white and pink and open to more than 4 inches wide. This crinum grows 2 to 3 feet tall and blooms in late summer.

planting and care

Select a partially shaded area with moist, rich soil. Plant bulbs with their necks above the soil level. Once your crinum plants are established, avoid moving them. If you do lift them, they may not bloom again for several years. Because of its fussiness about relocation, crinum is best grown in a container. In fact, the plant seems to thrive when pot bound. Plant one bulb in a 6-inch pot; cover all of the bulb except the tip with soil. Water and place the container in an area that receives at least four hours of sunlight per day. Remove the flowers from blooming plants as they fade. After the flowering stops, allow the foliage to wither and brown. Be sure to move the crinum indoors before frost.

crocosmia

For an exotic late-summer treat in your garden, plant the showy crocosmia. Commonly known as montbretia, its trumpet-shaped orange, red, yellow, or copper-colored flowers practically explode from bud-covered branching stems. These tropical beauties make superb container plants and add long-lasting vibrant color to beds and borders. Grown from corms, like gladiolus, crocosmia looks best when planted in groups of 10 to 12 bulbs. The flowers last for several weeks.

selecting crocosmia for your garden

Here's a list of commonly available crocosmia for your garden:

C. masoniorum, Zones 7–11 Growing 2 to 4 feet tall and blooming in July and August, this crocosima has orange, double rows of flowers. The foliage is sword shaped and showy. Plant in the full sun. 'Lucifer,' a popular variety, grows 15 to 20 inches tall and blooms in midsummer.

C. x crocosmiiflora (Common Montbretia), Zones 7–11 This hybrid grows to heights of 4 feet and sports exotic red or yellow blooms that span 2 inches. It blooms in late summer and does best in full sun.

planting and care

Plant crocosmia corms in light, sandy soil, 3 to 4 inches deep and 3 to 4 inches apart. For the best effect, plant them in groups of 10 to 12 corms. In southern states, mulch well so the corms survive the moderate winters. In areas that receive frost, lift the corms and store them. In the fall, after the flowers fade, allow the foliage to wither and yellow. Carefully dig the corms from the ground with a garden shovel or fork. Clean the soil from the corms gently, and clip away yellow foliage. Allow them to dry for a week in a cool place. Store the corms in a dry, cool, but frost-free place. Replant the following spring.

eucomis

The flower spikes of eucomis are like no other bulb bloom. Appropriately called the pineapple lily, the eucomis plant produces large, sword-shaped leaves with a flowered spike that resembles a pineapple—complete with topknot. Eucomis does well in both perennial borders or in containers and is quick to bloom; it takes the bulbs less than two months after planting. Growing 1 to 3 feet tall, the spikes produce white, pink, or green flowers, depending on the variety, and make stunning flower arrangements.

selecting eucomis for your garden

Here's a list of commonly available eucomis for your garden:

E. bicolor (Pineapple Lily), Zones 7–11 A South African native, this species grows 12 to 15 inches tall. The large spikes have delicate burgundy–veined white flowers topped with a showy hat of green foliage. A real showstopper, *E. bicolor* looks wonderful in containers.

E. comosa (Pineapple flower), Zones 7–11 Reaching heights of 1 to 2 feet, the elegant pineapple flower spire has delicate green-tinged, ½-inch flowers lined up in rows, crowned with a leafy-green topknot. Blooming in midsummer, these tender beauties do best in full sun.

planting and care

Select a well-drained spot that receives full sun. Plant the bulbs so their necks are just below the soil. In southern gardens, eucomis can remain in the ground all year. In areas north of Zone 7, eucomis overwinters indoors. If the plants are in a container, move them inside before the weather turns cold. If your eucomis is in a border or bed, dig the bulbs before frost using a garden fork. Allow them to dry, and clip off the foliage. Store the bulbs in vermiculite until spring, then replant them in the garden or pot in a container.

freesia

Freesia is a standard in most florist arrangements because of its many-hued flowers and
lovely fragrance. With blooms of purple,
orange, rose, pink, yellow, and white, freesia
can perform the same magic in your garden.
Fragrant, colorful, and full of flowers, they are
a welcome addition to any bed or border. A
dividend is that you can create the most wonderful bouquets for yourself. A native of South
Africa, freesia blooms in both single- and
double-flowering varieties. One bulb generally
produces two stems, both of which are covered
with a multitude of buds.

selecting freesia for your garden

F. x hybrida, Zones 9–11 Blooming in nearly all colors of the rainbow, freesia hybrids also are available in single- and double-petaled 2-inch flowers. Their swordlike foliage reaches heights of 1½ to
2 feet.

planting and care

In the late spring when the soil temperature is safely above 60 degrees Fahrenheit, plant the corms. It's
best to set the corms into the ground as early as your location will allow. Freesia does best in the cool
weather of late spring, but at the same time, it is tender and will not tolerate cold weather. Plant freesia
corms 1 to 2 inches apart, about 1 to 2 inches beneath the soil's surface. For the best effect, plant them
in groups of 10 to 20 corms.

In the South, freesia corms can remain in the ground all season; in the North, the corms must be
lifted and stored indoors. For this reason, freesia is best grown in pots in the North.

galtonia

The white-flowered, trumpet-shaped spires of galtonia bloom in mid- to late summer. Commonly called summer hyacinth, galtonia earns its nickname from its tall spires of fragrant, airy blooms.

Although not as stocky or packed with blooms as the spring-blooming hyacinth, galtonia produces lovely 2- to 3-foot flower stalks with attractive 2-inch nodding flowers. Underused in most gardens, galtonia looks great grouped with equally tall perennials in the back of a border. Sun-loving galtonia also is an excellent choice for containers.

selecting galtonia for your garden

G. candicans (Summer hyacinth), Zones 6–11 The only commonly available galtonia species, *G. candicans*, sometimes is sold as sold as *Hyacinthus candicans*. The 2- to 3-foot-tall stalks of summer hyacinth rise from attractive strap-shaped leaves and are topped with showy, white, drooping flowers. This South African native is slightly hardier than other summer bulbs and will tolerate cool weather if well mulched.

planting and care

Select a well-drained spot that receives full sun. Plant the bulbs 6 inches deep. To bolster blooms, enrich the soil with well-aged compost. In southern gardens, galtonia can be left in the ground all year, although it benefits from a 2-inch layer of mulch over the winter. In fact, galtonia can overwinter in the ground up to Zone 6 with heavy mulch. In colder climates, lift the bulbs and store them indoors for the winter. Dig the bulbs before frost using a garden fork, and allow them to dry. Separate offsets from the bulbs for planting in the spring. Clip off the withered foliage, and store the bulbs in vermiculite until spring, when you can replant them in the garden or a container.

gloriosa

True to its name, the gloriosa lily truly is glorious. It's a climber, too. In fact, it's one of the only bulbs that develops into a vine. Native to the tropics, these handsome plants show off in gardens in only the warmest regions. Trailing to lengths of 8 to 12 feet, gloriosa can be started in greenhouses or set in the ground and lifted before frost for northern gardeners. Their exquisite flowers are lovely in arrangements as well.

selecting gloriosa for your garden

Here's a list of commonly available gloriosa for your garden:

G. superba, Zones 10–11 The twisted yellow blooms of this species are tipped with deep red as they mature. Growing to 12 feet, the vine does best in full sun. This beauty looks stunning on a trellis when it is in full bloom in midsummer.

G. rothschildiana, Zones 3–11 Trailing to 8 feet, this tropical climber does best in full sun. The 3-inch-wide red and yellow flowers of *G. rothschildiana* start to appear in midsummer. The exquisite blooms are lovely in cut-flower arrangements, but take care when handling them because pollen shaken from the long stamens stains clothing and skin.

planting and care

Plant gloriosa tubers in a well-drained garden bed or in a container. These showy climbers require a sheltered spot that receives full sun. Do not plant outdoors until the weather is reliably above 60 degrees Fahrenheit. Plant the tubers 4 to 5 inches deep and leave 8 to 12 inches between each tuber. Be sure to provide a trellis at planting time for support. In the warmest areas of the country, gloriosa can remain in the ground all winter. In cold-weather locations, lift temperature-sensitive tubers before the first frost. Using a garden fork, carefully dig the tubers and store them in dry vermiculite in a cool, frost-free location until spring.

hymenocallis

The unusual, fragrant blooms of hymenocallis almost defy description. A collar of wispy petals surrounds a daffodillike trumpet from which gold-tipped stamens burst forth. Commonly called Peruvian daffodil and spider lily, hymenocallis is related to the amaryllis, whose wonderful family trait of beautiful flowers and lush, straplike foliage is carried on by this plant. Blooming in white or yellow, hymenocallis sometimes is sold as Ismene.

selecting hymenocallis for your garden

Here's a list of commonly available hymenocallis for your garden:

H. caribaea, Zones 10–11 Growing on stems that reach 3 feet tall, this species has white, explosive blooms that do best in sunny to partially shaded areas. Expect flowers in late spring to early summer.

H. narcissiflora (Basket flower, Peruvian daffodil), Zones 3–11 This is the most commonly available hymenocallis. Named for its similarity in looks to the daffodil, *H. narcissiflora* has ribbonlike petals surrounded by a trumpet with long, spidery stamens. Growing 2 feet tall, this species is a good choice for perennial borders or pots.

planting and care

Select a well-drained, sunny location. Plant the bulbs 3 to 5 inches deep, allowing 9 to 12 inches between bulbs. In the South, hymenocallis can overwinter in the ground. In the North, lift the bulbs carefully with a garden fork before frost. Allow them to dry completely. When the foliage is dead, clip off the leaves and store the bulbs in dry sphagnum peat moss or vermiculite in a frost-free location. Replant them in spring once frost no longer is a threat.

ixia

Also called corn bells, corn lilies, and wandflower, ixia grows 15 to 17 inches tall and bears spikes of showy blooms. The six-petaled, starlike flowers are available in a wide range of colors, including cream, yellow, purple, and rose. Ixia flowers are 1½ inches wide and have a contrasting color at the base of each petal. Flowering in July and August, ixia blooms on tall, slender stems, which make it a superb cut flower. Long-lived in a vase or the garden, ixia holds its bloom for about three weeks. Thriving best in warm climates, ixia has corms that must be lifted each winter in northern gardens.

selecting ixia for your garden

I. hybrids, Zones 7–11 Flowering in a wide range of vibrant colors, most with a deeper colored eye, ixia hybrids have grass-like, slender foliage. Planted in a mixed group of colors, ixia infuses midsummer color in the garden.

planting and care

Plant ixia in a sunny spot. The soil should be well-drained and the location well-protected. Add compost to enrich the soil for better bloom show. Plant the corms 4 inches deep and 3 to 4 inches apart. Ixia does well in containers, too; plant four to seven corms per pot at the same depth as outdoor planting. If you want ixia flowers for cutting, plant them in the garden in rows to facilitate harvesting. Don't overlook their presence in a perennial bed or border, however, where their marvelous bloom stalks provide late-summer color. In the South, ixia can overwinter in the ground, but protect the tender corms with a heavy mulch. In the North, lift ixia corms and store them in a frost-free location for the winter.

nerine

Nerine is named for a mythical Greek sea nymph. Its frothy, waving blooms add a graceful element to container gardens and perennial borders. Sometimes referred to as Guernsey lilies, these amaryllis family members reach 2 feet tall and produce exotic pink blossoms atop leafless stems. This late-summer bloomer looks stunning in a protected border where its topheavy blooms are safe from the wind. In the North, try them in containers.

selecting nerine for your garden

Here's a list of commonly available nerine for your garden:

N. bowdenii, Zones 9–11   The most commonly available nerine species, *N. bowdenii* produces striking dark rose blooms that measure 3 inches wide. Growing atop slender, leafless stalks reaching heights of 18 to 20 inches, these late-summer bloomers excel in garden borders and can easily be grown in containers. You can force nerine indoors.

N. sarniensis (Guernsey lily), Zones 9–11   Although not a native of Guernsey (the bulbs reportedly arrived on the shores of Guernsey after a shipping accident), *N. sarniensis* is instead from South Africa. Growing to heights of 2 feet, this late-summer bloomer is perfect for a mixed-flower border.

planting and care

Nerine does best in rich, loose soil, so prepare the bed with soil amendments such as compost. Set the bulbs in holes 4 inches deep. The bulbs bloom in late summer or early fall. In the South, you can leave nerine in the ground all year. In the North, dig the tender bulbs and store them inside in a frost-free location. Because these bulbs are so sensitive to temperatures, you may prefer to plant them in pots, which are easier to bring indoors than lifting the bulbs each year.

ornithogalum

Spring isn't the only time you can enjoy ornithogalum. One species, *O. saundersiae*, produces white, baseball-sized blooms borne on 3- to 4-foot-tall stems during summer. Resembling white alliums, the flowers of this ornithogalum are composed of many small blooms, each dotted with a striking dark eye. Hardy in warm zones, this bulb can be lifted in the fall and stored for replanting in the spring.

selecting ornithogalum for your garden

O. saundersiae, Zones 7–10 Commonly called the star of good hope and giant chincherinchee, this showy bulb is best planted at the back of the border. The large, waving balls of bloom make a wonderful backdrop for smaller perennials when planted in groups of three to five bulbs scattered throughout the border.

planting and care

In the spring after the threat of frost has passed, plant the bulbs 1 inch deep in sandy soil. Select a protected place so the blooms will not be pummeled by the wind. Blooming in late summer, *O. saundersiae* can remain in the ground all winter in the South. In colder zones, lift the bulbs using a garden fork. Allow them to dry, and remove the foliage. Store the bulbs in a cool, dry location free from frost. In the spring, replant the bulbs.

oxalis

Even if you've never heard of oxalis before, you've certainly seen them dressed up in green ribbons and sold to celebrate St. Patrick's Day. Although unrelated to shamrocks, the foliage of oxalis are shamrock-shaped, making the plants attractive even when out of bloom. Although its common name is wood

sorrel, you'll find many who still mistakenly call this plant a shamrock. Depending on the variety, oxalis is either green- or burgundy-leaved and bears delicate pink or white nodding blooms that hover delicately above the plant.

selecting oxalis for your garden

Here's a list of commonly available oxalis for your garden:

O. deppei, Zones 8–10 The common names associated with this plant make you wonder if you can ward off mishaps by having one growing at your home. Names such as good-luck plant and lucky clover help along the association oxalis has with the shamrock. You don't need the luck of the Irish to fall in love with this plant, however. Green, clover-shaped leaves are topped with hovering bright pink flowers. Growing 8 to 10 inches tall, this plant is beautiful in a pot or growing in a shady spot in your garden.

O. regnelli, Zones 8–10 This species often is called shamrock, too. White or pink flowers are a lovely contrast to its deep burgundy foliage. It grows 8 to 10 inches high and blooms in July and August.

planting and care

Although you most often see oxalis growing in a pot (all except *O. violacea* can be grown indoors as houseplants), you also can plant them directly in the garden. They prefer sun or partial shade and bloom in midsummer. To grow them in containers, plant at least three or four corms to produce a nice clump. When the danger of frost threatens, move the plants, pot and all, to a sunny window indoors.

polianthes

A popular cut flower with an intoxicating fragrance, polianthes is a valuable ingredient in the most sensuous perfumes. Its white clustered blooms will cast its fragrant magic over your garden as well. Commonly known as tuberose, polianthes grows 18 to 20 inches tall and blooms in both single- and double-flowering varieties. Native to Mexico, polianthes is one of the last summer bulbs to bloom, but it is worth the wait. A very tender bulb, tuberoses must be dug up before frost in the North.

selecting polianthes for your garden

P. tuberosa (Tuberoses), Zones 7–10 This species is the only commonly available polianthes. Blooming in both single and double forms, enjoy this fragrant flower in bouquets.

Single flowering Clusters of trumpet-shaped blooms release wafts of lovely perfume. Superb as a cut flower because of its fragrance, single-flowered polianthes also are long-lasting. The charming white blooms make an elegant statement alone in a vase, or mixed with an arrangement of other late-summer flowers.

Double flowering The waxy, thick-petaled blooms of double-flowering polianthes grow on 30-inch-tall stems. 'The Pearl' is a popular variety.

planting and care

In late spring, after the threat of frost has safely passed, find a sunny spot to plant polianthes. The soil should be well-drained and on the sandy side. Set the bulbs in a hole 3 inches deep, and allow 4 to 5 inches between each. To ensure the best bloom, water generously and nourish with a well-balanced fertilizer at least once a month. Stagger planting times for constant bloom.

Because they are inexpensive, you may want to treat garden polianthes as annuals and replace them each year. If you want to use the same bulbs next year, lift them, allow them to dry for several days, and store the bulbs in a cool, frost-free location.

ranunculus

The flowers of ranunculus look as if they're made of crepe paper, which makes them a favorite of florists and gardeners alike. Available in both single- and double-flowering varieties, blooms range in size from 1 to 4 inches wide. Most impressive are the double blooms, which are solidly packed with petals. Ranunculus blooms in a wide palette of colors, including white, red, yellow, orange, and pink. Newer varieties offer the largest flowers and the color range. Reaching heights of 12 to 14 inches, the lush blossoms start appearing in July and August. Each ranunculus bulb produces six to eight flowers at intervals of one or two weeks, so you'll have lots of flowers for show and cutting.

selecting ranunculus for your garden

R. asiaticus (Persian buttercup), Zones 8-10 The perfect double flowers of *R. asiaticus* are the choice of florists. Blooming during early summer, these plants produce a large number of blooms for nearly two months. The flowers are available in nearly all colors of the rainbow except blue.

planting and care

Start ranunculus indoors in a greenhouse in the late spring, or set them directly outdoors when the danger of frost has passed. Soak the stiff, dry tubers in warm water for several hours before planting to encourage sprouting. Set the tubers 2 inches deep with their points pointing down. Ranunculus demands plenty of sun and a fertile, well-drained, but not continually dry, location. Group 10 to 20 ranunculus bulbs together in the same spot for a bold show of bloom. In the fall, after the foliage has died back, lift the bulbs. Store them through the winter in boxes of sphagnum peat moss or perlite in a cool, dry location that stays 50 to 55 degrees Fahrenheit.

sparaxis

If you like the elegance of gladiolus, you'll want to try sparaxis. Upright and statuesque, these plants produce 12- to 18-inch spikes of flowers. The six-petaled flowers bloom in red, yellow, purple, and white, and most have contrasting dark color at the throat, giving them a wonderful pinwheel appearance. These magical-looking plants earn two appropriately descriptive common names: wandflower, for its upright growth habit, and harlequin, for its dramatic coloring. Blooming in early summer, sparaxis grows best in sunny areas. Sparaxis does well in containers and is an excellent cut flower.

selecting sparaxis for your garden

S. tricolor, Zones 7–11 Growing to 18 inches with sword-shaped leaves, *S. tricolor* produces 1- to 2-inch-wide flowers in white and red-orange. Tender natives of South Africa, these temperature-sensitive corms do best in south-facing, well-protected locations.

planting and care

Plant the corms in the spring once the ground has warmed. Select a sunny, well-protected area. Sparaxis does best in dry, well-drained soil, and thrive marvelously in locations that have dry summers. Dig holes 2 to 3 inches deep and place the corms 2 to 3 inches apart. To create the showiest display of sparaxis, plant a mixed clump of 10 or more bulbs. The blooms last about one week.

In warm areas, sparaxis can overwinter in the ground. In the North, lift sparaxis corms and store in a frost-free location for the winter. In areas that receive a lot of rain in the summer, sparaxis is best planted in containers, which makes them easier to move indoors when the weather changes.

tigridia

Native to Mexico and other areas of Central America and South America, tigridia produces extremely exotic blooms. Its common names, tiger flower and Mexican shell flower, attempt to describe the unusual characteristics of this plant. Each bloom has a bowllike form with a dappled center. Surrounded by sword-shaped leaves, the stems of tigridia rise to 1 to 2 feet tall. The 5- to 6-inch, three-petaled blooms come in red, yellow, white, orange, and pink.

selecting tigridia for your garden

T. pavonia, Zones 8–11 Extremely exotic looking, this species grows 1 to 2 feet tall. Its luscious, deeply colored flowers open 5 to 6 inches wide, exposing a decorative, dappled center. Although the blooms last just one day, each stem produces many flowers over the summer.

planting and care

After the threat of spring frosts have passed, plant tigridia in sunny or partially shaded locations. Dig a hole 4 inches deep, and space the bulbs 4 to 6 inches apart. Tigridia does best if well watered and fed with a well-balanced fertilizer throughout the summer. In warmer areas, tigridia can remain in the ground over winter. In the North, lift the bulbs after the leaves have withered. With a garden fork, carefully lift the bulbs and shake off excess soil. Allow them to dry for a few days, then store them in a box of peat moss or vermiculite. Make sure the storage location is free of frost. In spring, replant the bulbs when the soil warms.

zephyranthes

Zephyranthes goes by many common names, including zephyr lily, rain lily, and fairy lily. Named for the west wind, the zephyr lily is a true native of North America. The plant's common name fairy lily perhaps best describes how delightful and spritelike these tiny flowers look in a rock garden, perennial border, or small container. Growing to 1 foot tall, zephyranthes species bloom from early to late summer. Grasslike foliage surrounds the crocus-shaped blooms, which are available in white, yellow, or rose, depending on the species.

selecting zephyranthes for your garden

Here's a list of commonly available zephyranthes for your garden:

Z. atamasco (Atamasco lily, fairy lily), Zones 7–11 The hardiest of all zephyranthes species, *Z. atamasco* produces delicate white flowers that measure 2 to 3 inches long. Growing to 1 foot tall, this species blooms in early summer.

Z. grandiflora (Zephyr lily), Zones 9–11 This plant's 3-inch pink or rose blooms open on 12-inch stalks. The star-shaped blooms require full sun for best effect. Growing on leafless stems, it's easy to see the amaryllis family influence. The lily blooms in late spring and early summer.

planting and care

In the spring, once the ground has warmed, select a planting location. Enrich the bed with sphagnum peat moss and compost before planting. Set the bulbs in a hole 1 to 2 inches deep, and allow 2 to 3 inches between bulbs. Once flowering, zephyranthes will hold its bloom for more than a week. In the South, you can leave the bulbs in the ground over the winter; for added protection, mulch the garden bed. In colder areas, lift the bulbs and store them indoors over the winter. Store them in a cool, dry place as you would gladiolus.

fall

When the luster of your summer

bulbs has waned and the brilliance

of your perennial border is fading,

look to fall-flowering bulbs to

resurrect your garden's beauty.

With their almost mystical quality,

bulbs such as lycoris, colchicum,

fall crocus, and sternbergia rise and

shine, illuminating the autumn garden

with renewed vigor and color.

In a brilliant swan song of bloom,

these persistent bulbs continue

flowering beyond the first frosts.

lily, Oriental

Oriental lilies exhibit the best of what bulbs offer. Their blooms are large, luscious, colorful, and sweetly fragrant. And, like loyal friends, their companionship in the garden each autumn is guaranteed. Unlike other bulbs that bloom in late summer and early autumn, Oriental lilies are large, loud, and flamboyant. You can practically hear the brassy sounds of their long, open trumpets as they swing in fall breezes atop tall, sturdy stalks. Oriental hybrids add lavish splashes of color to your garden when the heat and sun have taken their toll on summer-blooming bulbs and perennials. Multiblossomed and long lasting, these stunning flowers are unequaled whether arranged in a mixed bouquet of late-summer perennials or as a single dramatic bloom in a vase.

Oriental lilies generally are hybrids of *Lilium auratum* and *L. speciosum*. Thanks to extensive hybridization, varieties of these lilies begin blooming in June and finish up in late September. Early bloomers generally are smaller than the autumn flowers, which are magnificent in both height and size of blooms. Planted in the fall, Oriental lilies are most dramatic when they infuse new color in the garden at the end of the summer.

selecting Oriental lilies for your garden

Some well-known varieties are 'Casa Blanca,' 'Stargazer,' 'Le Reve,' 'Imperial Silver,' and 'Jamboree.' All grow in Zones 3–9. Catalogs and garden centers are filled with a wonderful spectrum of colors of Oriental lilies. Certainly the most artistic

'Casa Blanca' lilies, right, probably are one of the most spectacular lilies you can grow. For best effect, plant in groups of three or more, spacing bulbs 8 inches apart. Here, the plants' snow-white blooms contrast nicely with pink phlox.

lilies, Oriental lilies appear to have been hand-painted with joyous excess. Petals bear spots, stains, and splashes of color with wild abandon. Single-colored blooms have rich, reverberating tones. Even the stamens are richly colored. Flower form varies greatly: Some open outward in great exaggerated sweeps, while others are flat with a flirtatious petal ripple. Oriental lilies' lofty stature is another element of their imposing stage presence in the garden. Towering to 6 feet tall and multiflowered, these fantastic plants scent the garden from great heights.

Pure-white 'Casa Blanca' blooms in early August and has 6-inch flowers. 'Imperial Silver,' also snow white, has delicate red

No garden is really complete unless it has a generous helping of Oriental lilies. 'Laura Lee,' left, provides plenty of dramatic color during the dog days of August. Planted amid hosta and hydrangea, 'Casa Blanca,' below, is a winner.

dots covering its slightly arching petals and its blazing crimson stamens. 'Stargazer,' a popular Oriental lily, is crimson and white. The soft pink 'Le Reve' is lightly spotted with a hint of yellow at the base of its petals. 'Imperial Crimson' and 'Jamboree' are crimson spotted with darker red and trimmed in crisp white edges. Although most Oriental lilies bloom in rich color ranges of white, pink, and crimson (and exotic combinations of all three), there also are white varieties tinged with deep gold, such as *L. auratum* 'platyphyllum.'

Towering over other flowers in the perennial border, 'Imperial Pink,' opposite, commands plenty of attention when its pink petals unfurl. Because it can grow 4 to 5 feet tall, be sure to plant 'Imperial Pink' in the back of the border with other tall varieties.

planting and care

Oriental lilies can be planted in spring or early fall. Before you plant, be sure your bed is in good condition and receives at least five to six hours of sun each day. Till or spade the bed and rake the surface smooth. Lilies require well-drained soil so the bulbs don't rot. If the soil is too wet, add sand to increase drainage. Dig a hole about 1 foot deep, and place the lily bulb in the bottom. Oriental lilies are most stunning in small groups, so plant them in clumps of at least three bulbs.

In spring, add fertilizer to the soil around the plants to bolster blooms. Select varieties for their bloom time so you can stagger their flowering throughout the summer. If you plan it right, you can have Oriental lilies blooming in your garden from June to August. Once the flowers are at their peak, make sure to clip some for indoor bouquets. When plants have finished flowering, reduce watering and allow them to stand undisturbed. When the clumps become too thick, dig and divide the bulbs.

To grow lilies in large containers, layer aluminum cans on the bottom to keep the pot lightweight. Then add soil.

Set your lily bulbs on top of the soil; using three bulbs per 16-inch pot. Cover with more soil and add a wire plant support.

lycoris

Named for the mistress of Marc Anthony, lycoris lends seductiveness to any garden. These tall, bare-legged beauties wear exotic crowns of blooms that boldly scent your garden while adding an element of intrigue to a border. Lycoris also blooms happily in pots, so you can place the beautiful blooms anywhere to fit your moods and whims. With a wide variety of colors to choose from, you should relegate the elegant lycoris to its own special place in the garden. Lycoris blooms in white, yellow, pink, and purple.

selecting lycoris for your garden

Here's a list of commonly available lycoris for your garden:

L. radiata (Red spider lily), Zones 7–11 This stunning variety sports red blooms borne on leafless 16-inch stems. The ½-inch blooms have long, slender stigmas that form an airy cup around its petals. Half-hardy, lycoris does best in warmer climates. For a different color mix, try *L. albiflora* (white spider lily) or *L. africana* (golden spider lily).

L. squamigera (Magic lily, resurrection lily), Zones 5–11 The common names resurrection lily and magic lily attest to the wondrous appearance this lycoris species presents in the garden. In early spring, leaves emerge, then wither and die back within several weeks. In the fall, 1- to 2-foot stems crowned with pink trumpets rise from the rubble. Fragrant and very showy, these beauties are an unexpected delight scattered throughout your perennial border. Lycoris naturalizes well, so plant in a place where it can spread its glory.

planting and care

L. radiata can be planted in late summer. Select a spot that receives full sun, such as an existing perennial bed or border. Because it is tall, it looks best in the back of the border. The soil should be well drained. Place the bulbs in the soil so their tips are just below the surface.

L. squamigera is best planted in early autumn. Select a spot that receives partial sun. The soil should be well drained. Add sand to increase drainage if necessary. Dig a hole about 4 to 5 inches deep, place the bulbs in the hole, and cover with soil. If you want to divide and replant the bulbs, do so in the spring after the foliage has withered.

colchicum

The soft purple blooms of colchicum rise from the ground on bare stems during the last throes of summer. So startling are these undressed plants, that they are nicknamed "naked boys." Also called meadow saffron and autumn crocus, colchicum is very crocuslike in appearance, although it bears larger flowers and has more stamens than the crocus.

Like many other fall-flowering bulbs, colchicum's leaves appear in the spring and die back over the summer, and the flowers bloom in the fall. Growing 6 to 8 inches tall, the translucent pink petals seem to capture the last of summer's light in their cup-shaped blooms. Lovely in the garden border, tucked into a rock garden, or poking through fallen leaves in a woodland, colchicum does equally well in full sun or partially sunny areas.

selecting colchicum for your garden

Here's a list of commonly available colchicum for your garden:

C. autumnale, Zones 4–11 This, most common colchicum, is native to Europe and northern Africa. Plants achieve heights of 8 to 10 inches. Generally, blooms are soft pink with hints of lilac, but 'Album' is a white single variety, and a double variety blooms in pink or white. 'Waterlily,' a stunning double lilac variety (pictured above), is widely available.

planting and care

Colchicum provides almost instant gratification because it will bloom the same season ity is planted. So eager are these bulbs to bloom that they'll do just that without benefit of either water or soil. In fact, you can place a colchicum corm on a sunny windowsill, and it will sprout and flower.

In late summer, select a sunny to partially shaded spot for your colchicum. Dig a hole 2 to 3 inches deep, place the corms in the hole, and cover with soil. Within weeks flowers emerge, hold their bloom, then vanish. The following spring, leaves sprout, grow, then die back during the summer. You must allow the leaves to grow and wither so the corms can gather strength for future blooms.

crocus, fall

Fall-blooming crocus is a welcome sight in the long shadow of late summer. Cup-shaped flowers top leafless stalks, as they stubbornly push their way through leaf litter and dying plants. As eager to naturalize as their spring-blooming cousins, fall crocus will wander and spread with delight. Almost in denial of the coming winter, these vigorous little charmers are tough enough to withstand early frosts, boldly blooming through light snows.

selecting crocus for your garden

Here's a list of commonly available fall-blooming crocus for your garden:

C. longiflorus, Zone 5 Both the ribbonlike foliage and the yellow-throated lilac bloom of this crocus emerge from the ground at the same time. Blooming in late fall to heights of 5½ inches, these crocuses will return each year to usher in winter in style.

C. medius, Zones 6–7 The bright lilac blooms of this crocus emerge before the foliage. Growing 4 to 10 inches tall, this hardy crocus is prolific in blooms and its ability to naturalize.

C. sativus, Zones 6–9 The best-known fall crocus is *C. sativus.* Dear in price and coveted for its seasoning and coloring abilities, saffron is harvested from the dried stigmas of this easy-to-grow variety. Plants grow 3 to 6 inches tall.

planting and care

The best thing about fall-blooming crocuses is they bloom the same season you plant them. Planted in the late summer, they unfurl their delicate flowers weeks after you set them in the ground. Place corms 2 inches apart, in a hole 2 to 4 inches deep. The soil should be amended with bonemeal or a balanced fertilizer after planting. Because these hardy bulbs are inexpensive and easy to naturalize, be generous when you plant them. Fall-blooming crocuses multiply prolifically, and you'll be rewarded with large clumps of blooms that increase in size each year.

cyclamen, hardy

You've probably received a cyclamen at least once in your life as a gift plant, but there are other species of cyclamen that flourish outdoors. Commonly called alpine violet, cyclamen is hardy in warmer regions. Small and delicate, cyclamen's blooms accent any rock garden or border plantings. These shade-tolerant beauties flower in spring or fall. For fall planting, you'll find several species to choose from all of which bloom in crisp lipstick colors of white, pink, rose, and lilac. Growing 3 to 6 inches tall, cyclamen really is only half-hardy, meaning it will return in warmer climates but is too tender for more frigid areas.

selecting cyclamen for your garden

Here's a list of commonly available cyclamen for your garden:

C. cilicium, Zones 6–9 The lovely flowers of cyclamen resemble delicate butterflies in flight, suspended in midair above heart-shaped green-and-silver leaves. Look for the fragrant, light pink blooms of this cyclamen to appear from September to November. Plant in a partially shaded area in dry, gritty soil for the best bloom.

C. hederifolium, Zones 7–9 A native to southern Europe, its heart-shaped leaves sit below pink or white blooms marked with a brilliant drop of crimson.

C. purpurascens Zones 7-9 Growing 3 to 6 inches tall, this fragrant cyclamen sports dark pink blooms that hover on thin stems above variegated leaves.

planting and care

Cyclamen can be planted in spring or fall. Hardy cyclamen does best in partially shaded areas in well-drained soil that is on the sandy, gritty side. If the soil is too wet, add sand to make it more suitable. Plant the bulbs ½ inch deep and allow 6 to 8 inches between them. When the bulbs have flowered, let the leaves yellow and wither without disturbing them. Once established, the cyclamen does best when left alone. For winter preparation, mulch with peat moss or ground pine bark.

sternbergia

Like golden coins tossed amid the fallen leaves, the blooms of sternbergia are a surprising sight in the fall. Even after frost has claimed its spoils from the garden, sternbergia blooms on. Three species of sternbergia flower in the fall; two others bloom in the spring. The shining golden sternbergia with its chalicelike blooms looks spectacular in rock gardens or in the footlights of a perennial border. Growing only 6 inches tall, this cheery plant also is excellent planted in pots and brought indoors.

Sternbergia is an endangered species in the wild, so make sure you get your bulbs from a reputable bulb source. Harvesting bulbs from the wild could deplete natural sources.

selecting sternbergia for your garden

S. lutea (Winter daffodil), Zones 7–9 The common name, winter daffodil, is misleading because sternbergia looks more like a crocus than a daffodil, although it is unrelated to either. Growing 6 inches tall with 2-inch golden-yellow blooms, sternbergia blooms in the early fall, with foliage coming first. The foliage remains green all winter, then dies back in the spring.

planting and care

As soon as sternbergia bulbs are available in midsummer to late summer, set them in the ground. Select a spot that receives full sun to partial shade. The soil should be well drained; add sphagnum peat moss to improve drainage if necessary. Position the bulbs about 3 inches apart and 5 inches deep and cover with soil. If frost is common in your area, you might want to mulch over top with straw or leaves. Plant sternbergia where it can stretch its legs, because it multiplies and naturalizes well.

winter

Chase away the winter blues with containers of blooming forced bulbs. With a little planning, even a novice gardener can reap the harvest of fragrant and colorful hyacinths, narcissus, tulips, muscari, and other bulbs that flower indoors during the winter months. Forcing, the process of coaxing bulbs into thinking they have overwintered and are ready for spring, allows you to produce glorious blossoms when you need them most—in the dead of winter. Whether you pot them up for gift plants or hoard them all for yourself, the grandeur of forced bulbs is an easy and inexpensive way to brighten the dreary hues of winter.

amaryllis

When the showy amaryllis blooms, the explosion is visible from everywhere in a room. Bursting forth from tall stems, these robust plants grow to heights of 2 feet and produce three or four blossoms per stalk. From one bulb, a single, double, or triple set of stalks can emerge, all of which are crowned with flowers. The blooms are magnificent and can reach widths of 8 to 10 inches. Amaryllis is nearly fool-proof. They require no cold storage, as other forced bulbs do, and need only to be planted in a pot, placed in a sunny window, and watered.

Popular as winter and early spring holiday decorations and gift plants, amaryllis fits into any color scheme with its blooms that come in colors of white, pink, deep red, yellow, orange, and bicolors. Although the most expensive of all forcing bulbs, amaryllis also is the largest bulb and produces a lot of bloom for the money. Miniature varieties grow to 1½ to 2 feet and produce the same number of blossoms as their larger siblings. Double-flowered amaryllis is available in several colors. Although many sources sell amaryllis prepotted, complete with container, soil, and bulb, it's easy to pot it yourself. Either way, you'll be rewarded with stunningly spectacular blooms.

selecting amaryllis for your home

A wide array of amaryllis colors are available, ranging from deep, robust red to pristine snow white. Choose

Set amaryllis and paperwhite narcissus by a sunny window, and half the fun will be watching the flowers emerge in front of a wintry backdrop.

This entrancing cast of amaryllis includes 'Venus' (solid pink), 'Apple Blossom' (white with pink shades), 'Orange Star' (bright red-orange), and 'Milady' (pink with white stripes). Be sure to cut off the flower stalks when they fade.

Add to the magic of the holiday season with pots of blooming 'Apple Blossom' amaryllis. Their light pink flowers will last as long as three weeks. They also make great gifts. Just be sure to pot them about six weeks before you want them to flower.

planting and care

Amaryllis blooms five to eight weeks after you've planted it. Select a large, firm bulb that is free of bruises or blemishes. The bigger the bulb, the greater chance you have of getting multiple stalks of bloom. If you don't plan on potting up the bulb right away, store it in a well-ventilated, cool, dark spot with temperatures that safely range from 50 to 60 degrees. The pot should be twice as tall as the bulb to allow ample room for proper root growth. Fill it with a well-drained potting soil mixture high in sphagnum peat moss or vermiculite. Leave about one-third of the bulb above the soil. Make sure the bulb does not touch the edge of the pot or another bulb.

Tamp the soil down around the bulb and water, taking care not to soak the bulb. Although the soil should be moist, it should not be too wet or the bulb may rot instead of root. Place the potted amaryllis in a sunny window that has a temperature of 70 to 75 degrees F. Water sparingly until the bulb begins to sprout, then you should water just to maintain soil moisture.

Once the flowers open, move the plant away from its sunny spot to preserve the blooms. You may notice that the long stalks lean toward a sunny window, so to keep the plants from appearing lop-

Select a bulb that has a healthy root system. Gently untangle and separate the roots before planting.

'Red Lion' for cheery scarlet blooms that will accent holiday decorations. Multicolored amaryllis plants are regal and striking; try 'Apple Blossom,' a light pink-and-white variety, or 'Minerva,' a red-and-white flowering bulb.

To display your amaryllis plants, line them up on a fireplace mantel, a windowsill, or a front-entry table where they can make a welcoming statement. You can showcase amaryllis singly or combine them in a large planter with houseplants such as English ivy, ferns, or creeping fig. Avoid placing plants near drafts, radiators, and hot-air registers.

If the heavy blooms burden the stalks, stake your amaryllis before the flowers topple. For a rustic look, use twine to tie the bloom stalks to a bark-covered twig or branch. You also can buy commercial plant supports from nurseries, garden centers, and mail-order garden sources.

sided rotate the pot every week or two. If you pot up bulbs at 10-day intervals, you'll have continuous waves of bloom all winter. To keep your amaryllis for the following year, move it outdoors for a summer vacation to a spot that is protected from strong sunlight. In very warm climates, amaryllis can be planted outdoors year-round. Wait until the threat of frost has safely passed and sink the bulbs, pot and all, into a shady bed or border. When the foliage yellows in the fall, bring the bulbs back indoors for a two-month rest, then repot for another crop of winter blooms.

Soak roots in a shallow pan of luke-warm water for three to four hours before planting the bulb.

Suspend the bulb over the pot, then fill the pot with soil. Leave two-thirds of the bulb above the soil.

Place the pot near a sunny window or in a warm room with bright indirect light. Water to encourage growth.

lily-of-the-valley

The tiny, fragrant snow-white bells of convallaria, or lily-of-the-valley, ring in the start of spring in the garden. But why wait until the weather warms, when you can force them indoors. Special, pretreated bulbs, called pips, can be purchased from mail-order sources specifically for the purpose of forcing in any season. Growing 8 to 10 inches tall, the slender, delicate stalks hold 10 to 15 bell-shaped blooms that are as rich in fragrance as they are in folklore. Signifying happiness, lily-of-the-valley is nearly a standard in bridal bouquets. Nothing can more elegantly state joy than a tiny container filled with the arching, fragrant, flower-covered stalks of lily-of-the-valley.

selecting lily-of-the-valley for your home

The recommended species for forcing is *Convallaria majalis*. You generally can order lily-of-the-valley for forcing from catalogs. Check with your garden center manager to make sure the bulbs you are purchasing have been precooled and are suitable for indoor blooming.

Show off the pristine white blooms of lily-of-the-valley by planting them in white porcelain planters with delicate cutout edges. These plants also can dress up containers such as hand-painted china bowls, blue willow dishes, or a finely woven basket. For a country look, plant a clump of lily-of-the-valley in a rough-hewn wooden box or small wooden bread bowl with a soft blanket of Spanish moss.

planting and care

Lily-of-the-valley blooms three to four weeks after you've planted it. For the best results, select pretreated bulbs that have been precooled. Place the pips 1 to 2 inches apart and cover with 1 inch of soil. Water generously. In about three weeks you'll be rewarded with the elegant swordlike leaves and fragrant blooms. These delicate little beauties look best when planted in a clump, and bloom for 1½ weeks. Take special care with these plants because the bulbs are poisonous; keep them out of the reach of curious children and marauding pets.

narcissus

Containers of fragrant, flowering narcissus are wonderful sneak previews of spring, and a wide array of narcissus does well when forced. Hardy-blooming outdoor species herald springtime indoors with their vibrant trumpets. *N. tazetta*, commonly called paperwhite, is a tender species exclusively bred for indoor forcing. Easy to pot up and nearly 100 percent successful, paperwhites are also fragrant, filling a room with the scent and promise of spring.

selecting narcissus for your home

Paperwhites Choose either the white-flowering variety paperwhite 'Paper White Grandiflora' or the yellow bloomer 'Grand Soleil d'Or.' Paperwhites are most beautiful when a colony of bulbs is massed in one container. A feast for the eyes, a tabletop basket of luxuriant paperwhites is a warm sight in the cold winter. Each stem bears a ready-made bouquet of

Easy-to-grow bloomers will fill your home with sunny colors. The flowers near the window, right, include 'Einstein,' 'Dutch Master,' 'Early Splendor,' 'Kewpie Doll,' and 'Tête-à-Tête.'

A basket of 'Tête-à-Tête' narcissus, left, brightens dreary days with spring flowers. To create a paperwhite log, above, bend a piece of birch bark into the shape of a log and glue the edges together. Cut holes along one side of the log and set a pebble-filled, plastic saucer under each hole. Place bulbs on each saucer and add water.

four to eight delightfully fragrant, small white flowers with yellow cups.

Traditional narcissus   Dwarf or small narcissus is a good choice for indoor forcing. Varieties such as 'Jack Snipe' and 'Tête-à-Tête' produce small cheery blooms in bright yellow. 'February Gold' is another showstopper. Larger varieties also bloom well indoors. Combine pots of magnificent narcissus with other forced bulbs such as tulips or muscari to create an indoor window box. A well-placed container of narcissus can bring springtime to any room.

planting paperwhites

To grow paperwhites in soil, place about 16 bulbs in a 12-inch pot three-quarters full with soil.

When the bulbs are in place, add more soil until only the shoulders of the bulbs are visible. Water thoroughly.

Place the pot in a bright, cool room. When the stems are 2 inches tall, move the pot to a warmer location.

planting and care

paperwhite narcissus

Paperwhites bloom four to eight weeks after you've planted them. Requiring neither cold storage nor soil, paperwhites perform equally well for first-time indoor gardeners and those who have been forcing bulbs for years. In addition to growing paperwhites in soil, you also can place the bulbs in a low dish filled with gravel and water, or if you like, you can even force them in a plain glass of water. Because these tender bulbs flower only once, discard the bulbs once they have completed their show. For a continuous show of color, be sure to start new pots of bulbs every few weeks throughout the fall and winter.

Although paperwhites do not require a period of cold and darkness to bloom, it's still a good idea to start them in a cool, dark location. As the bulbs sprout, you can move them to a more prominent location in your home. If the bulbs are started in a warm spot, the flower stalks have a tendency to get leggy and flop over. Cool temperatures help promote stocky growth. If your plants do get tall, stake them with lightweight, bamboo plant stakes.

planting standard narcissus

Fill your pot half full with potting soil. Use a soil mix that retains moisture, but allows good drainage.

Place as many bulbs as you can, but don't let the bulbs touch. Their growing tips should be even with the top of the pot.

Water the bulbs thoroughly and label each pot with the planting date. Then, move them to cold storage.

standard narcissus

Forced narcissus blooms 15 to 17 weeks after you've planted them. If you purchase bulbs from a mail-order source, select those sold specifically for forcing. If you are hand-selecting bulbs at a garden center, look for firm, double-nosed bulbs. Choose a 6-inch or larger container and fill it with a well-drained potting mixture. Because you want a substantial clump of blooms, plant the bulbs close together, but do not allow them to touch each other or the sides of the container. Once the bulbs are planted, set them in a cool, dark place such as a basement, garage, or refrigerator. Narcissus needs cooling for 12 to 15 weeks to give the bulbs time to set an extensive root system.

Once you see roots poking out of the bottom of the pot, or growth at the top of the bulb, move the pot to a sunny spot. Don't move the potted bulbs into the light too soon. They need adequate cooling time before warming up; if cooled too briefly, the bulbs may sprout, but you will be disappointed with the bloom.

While the blossoms are open, water generously but without making the soil soggy. When the flowers are finished, you may want to save the bulbs to replant in your garden. Allow the foliage to ripen and yellow. When the threat of frost has passed, plant the bulbs at the appropriate depth in the garden.

tulip

The indomitably cheery blooms of forced tulips are a sure antidote to the emotional ravages of a relentless winter. Tulips bloom in almost any shade of bold, primary colors to soft pastels. Create an indoor window box by lining up several pots of tulips on a sill. Sprouting out of baskets or pots, the splendor of blooming tulips indoors signifies the coming of spring. If you are too impatient to precool bulbs, try 'Jingle Bells,' a variety you can force in water like hyacinths and paperwhite narcissus.

selecting tulips for your home

Triumph tulips are sold widely for forcing and come in wonderful colors. For soft pastels, plant 'Apricot Beauty,' a rich apricot hue, as its name implies, or 'Attila,' a lovely lavender tulip. For a little pizzazz, try 'Merry Widow,' a glowing red tulip with a broad white edge, or the all-red 'Bing Crosby.'

'Pax' or 'Snowstar' are two popular pure-white varieties.

Plan an indoor garden by forcing different-colored tulips and mix in other bulbs, such as crocus, amaryllis, and muscari. As in a border or bed, position tall species at the back and shorter species in the front. Because you can estimate the time of bloom, you can plan for some pots to come into bloom just as others are finishing up. An indoor bulb garden is a sure way to ward off the blues of winter. For a formal effect, let the containers be a unifying factor; use all terra-cotta or pots of a single color, white perhaps. If you want a more eclectic look, search out containers that vary in color and material. A grouping of white hyacinths growing out of a rustic tool box,

Stage a spectacular indoor show with a potted troupe of tulips. Good forcing varieties include 'Sweet Lady,' above, and 'Kees Nelis,' 'Pink Pixie,' 'Angelique,' 'Albury,' and 'Christmas Gold,' opposite.

positioned next to a willow basket of beaming red tulips, fronted by a mush-room box spilling over in neon-blue muscari creates a woodland garden indoors. The best thing about bulbs is that they are very adaptable to any container, and with any container garden, you have the flexibility of mobility so you can arrange blooms to suit your mood, the location, or the decor.

planting and care

Tulips bloom 14 to 16 weeks after planting. Select bulbs from your local garden center or mail-order source specifically identified for forcing. Although you can force any tulip bulbs, you'll have better luck with desig-nated varieties. Place the bulbs close together without touching in a pot; plant about six to eight bulbs for a nice clump of blooms. Allow 1 to 2 inch-es of space between bulbs. Cover with soil and water generously.

To fool the bulbs into thinking they've overwintered, store the bulbs in a spot that's dark and cool (about 40 to 50 degrees F). The bulbs will sprout, and when they've reached the height of 4 inches (in about 10 to 12 weeks), you can spring them into warmth and sunshine. You want the bulbs to warm up, but not overheat, which would inhibit their flowering potential. Keep the soil moist, but not wet, during this time. The plants will form buds, and they'll do best if positioned in bright light to really coax out the bloom. Once the tulips bloom, move them out of direct light to preserve the blooms for as long as possible.

When the flowers have faded, you can discard the bulbs or plant them in your garden outdoors. To save and replant the bulbs, clip the stem and dis-card the spent blooms. Then allow the leaves to wither and die naturally. During this dormant period, the bulb gathers its strength for next year's bloom. Once the leaves are dead, remove the bulbs from the soil and store in a cool spot. When spring arrives, plant outside.

crocus

Fool Mother Nature by forcing crocus into bloom before it premieres in gardens outdoors. Available in a wide range of colors, the exultant blooms of crocus brighten any corner of your home. Appearing on a windowsill, a kitchen counter, or a bedroom nightstand, the triumphant blooms of the compact and mirthful crocus create spring-inspired scenes for winter-weary gardeners who long to get their hands back into the soil.

selecting crocus for your home

The widely available *C. vernus*, or Dutch crocus, is a foolproof forcing choice. For lavender blooms, try 'Remembrance' and 'Flower Record.' The perky purple-and-white-striped crocus 'Pickwick' is a showstopper. And the pristine all-white bloom of 'Jean d'Arc' are a hopeful sight in the grips of winter. *C. chrysanthus*, snow crocus, also is a good forcing candidate and offers a bit more color. Try the blue 'Zenith' or 'Blue Peter.' For a burst of sunlight, try 'Goldilocks.'

planting and care

Crocus blooms eight to 10 weeks after planting. When buying bulbs from a mail-order source or garden center, look for varieties identified specifically for forcing. Choose bulbs that are large, firm, and free of nicks and holes. Keep in mind that the larger the bulb, the larger the bloom. Once you have your crocuses home, pot them up immediately so the corms do not dry out. Select a small container and fill it with potting soil. Place the crocus corms in the soil mixture close together with their tips just peeking out of the soil. Water and place the container in a cool, dark spot for six to 10 weeks. When the corms begin to sprout, move them to a warmer spot in direct sunlight.

Fill your pot almost to the top with potting soil. Press in crocus bulbs.

Cover the bulbs with soil, leaving only their growing tips visible. Water.

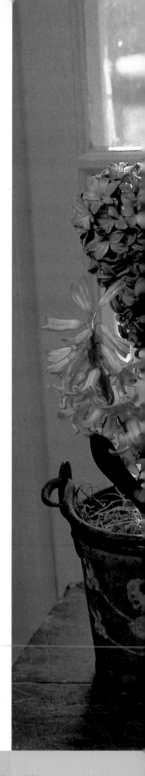

hyacinth

Even if your windows are frosted over with ice, you can enjoy the scents of spring with pots of blooming hyacinths scattered throughout your home. With little effort or gardening skill, you can have a pot of these perfumed lovelies in every room. The stocky hyacinth is the only bulb other than the amaryllis that looks as good planted singly as it does in a group.

selecting hyacinths for your home

The most popular hyacinth for forcing is *H. orientalis*, commonly known as a Dutch hyacinth. Growing 8 to 12 inches tall, the spiky hyacinth is available in a wide variety of colors. A good white hyacinth is 'Carnegie.' Try any of these blue-hued hyacinths for forcing: 'Delft Blue,' 'Blue Jacket,' and 'Ostara.' Red varieties include the double-flowered 'Hollyhock' and 'Jan Bos.' The lovely pink variety 'Anna-Marie' and the orange 'Gypsy Queen' are brilliant indoor bloomers.

Alone or planted in a group, the tall, uniform stature of hyacinths makes them great choices for a window box or large urn planters. Hyacinths are also lovely grouped with other pots of forced bulbs. For a striking still life of all-white blooms, group separate pots of 'Carnegie' hyacinths, 'Jean d'Arc' crocus, and 'Hibernia' triumph tulips.

planting and care

Hyacinths bloom eight to 13 weeks after planting. They are easy to force, because they bloom in a variety of media—in pebbles, soil, or water. Especially popular during the Victorian period, hyacinths were forced in water using a container called a hyacinth glass. A popular forcing method today, hyacinth glasses are hourglass-shape vases that allow the roots to be exposed to water while the bulb is kept dry and protected from rotting. Sprouting hyacinths this way especially appeals to children, who can behold the entire plant, roots and all.

To force hyacinths in a hyacinth glass (any narrow-necked jar will do fine as long as the bulb is not immersed in water), place a bulb, roots down, on the top of a water-filled container so bottom of bulb is in water. Make sure the base of the bulb just barely touches the surface of the water. Place in a dark, cool location until the bottom of the glass fills with roots. Then, move into the warmth and sunlight to activate the bloom process.

To force hyacinths in soil, follow the instructions for forcing standard narcissus on page 175.

muscari

Planted in shallow dishes, low-growing muscari makes stunning and unusual centerpieces. Occasionally overlooked in outdoor gardens, the diminutive, electric-blue muscari commands the spotlight when placed at center stage on a dining or coffee table.

selecting muscari for your home

The tiny beadlike blooms clustered like grapes deserve close attention because they are so singularly beautiful and fragrant. That means you can pot them up in small porcelain dishes, shallow serving bowls, or even teacups, then serve them up anywhere you need a burst of color. Or, bring the woodlands indoors by planting muscari in rough-hewn wooden troughs, plastic-lined willow baskets, or a rustic, weatherworn tin. Muscari are good mixers, so team them with dwarf narcissus such as 'Tête-à-Tête,' white crocus, or red tulips.

planting and care

Muscari bloom 10 to 14 weeks after planting. The best species of muscari to force is the blue *M. armeniacum*, which grows 8 to 10 inches tall. Precool the bulbs by sticking them into the refrigerator, sack and all, from the garden center. Allow at least eight weeks in cool storage. Late fall or midwinter, pull them out and pot them up. The bulb tips should be just below the surface of the soil. Because muscari are so small, pack in as many bulbs as you can without the edges touching. Give the planted bulbs a good soaking and then put them in a cool, dark place until they start to sprout. When shoots emerge through the soil's surface, move them to a warmer location where they will receive at least four hours of direct sunlight a day. Once the buds open, set the container in a cooler spot that receives filtered light so the flowers last longer.

gloxinia

When indoor-flowering tulips, narcissus, and muscari have faded, fill in the gaps with *Sinningia speciosa*, commonly called gloxinia. Capable of blooming anytime during the year, regal gloxinias produce rich, colored flowers. Exclusively cultivated for indoor gardening, gloxinia will not successfully transplant outdoors. But that's just as well, because you'll enjoy its tropical blooms better inside. Growing 8 to 12 inches tall, the soft, fragile-looking gloxinia blooms are surrounded by large, dramatic-looking leaves.

selecting gloxinia for your home

Because all varieties of gloxinia are tropical plants and do well only indoors, you can select the variety by flower color. Few indoor-blooming plants can boast the richness of color of the velvety trumpets of gloxinia. Flower colors include purple, purple edged with white, pure white, rose, rose edged with white, and mottled combinations.

Potted gloxinia can stand alone in elegance or be grouped together in a basket to form a large mound of bloom. The sometimes slipper-shaped flowers might seem to call for a refined container, but the rough, large leaves of the gloxinia look at home in more rustic surroundings, so you can go either way.

planting and care

Gloxinia blooms four to 10 weeks after you've planted it. If you are potting up a gloxinia for the first time, place one tuber per container. Use a 6-inch pot with adequate drainage. The soil mixture should allow maximum drainage; a commercial African violet mixture is good. Set the tuber in the soil with the round side down, and leave its tip barely above the soil. Water generously. Gloxinia does best in bright, but indirect, light and enjoy temperatures of 60 to 75 degrees F. When the first buds appear, feed with a dilute solution of liquid houseplant food.

design

Planning is the key to a beautiful bulb garden. Orchestrating blooming times, plant heights, and color combinations will make your garden a symphony of color all season. With our easy-to-plant garden plans included here, you can create a paint-by-the-numbers replica of an old master, or you can venture out on your own to create your personal tableau. Following the garden plans, you'll find valuable information about the tools you need for bulb gardening, plus a list of mail-order catalogs that sell bulbs and bulb-planting supplies. A zone map also is included to help you determine which species will do well in your climate.

The illustration labels read:

ESTELLA RIJNVELD
RENOWN
ESTELLA RIJNVELD
FANCY FRILLS
MIXED DOUBLE LATE
FANCY FRILLS
RED RIDING HOOD & ANEMONE BLANDA
BLUE MUSCARI
RED RIDING HOOD & ANEMONE BLANDA

double tulip border

The double border gets its name from the mixed plantings of 'Red Riding Hood' tulips and white anemone (*Anemone blanda*). To create these double drifts of color, it's important to choose varieties that bloom at the same time. Start by digging a hole deep enough to accommodate the larger bulbs, usually the tulips. Put the tulip bulbs in the hole and cover them with soil until you reach the appropriate level for smaller species such as anemone, crocus, and scilla. Then, set the smaller bulbs in place over the larger ones. Cover with the rest of the soil and water thoroughly. In the spring, both sets of bulbs will appear together, creating a spectacular display of color. In the garden above left, white crocus and red tulips were planted in this manner the previous autumn.

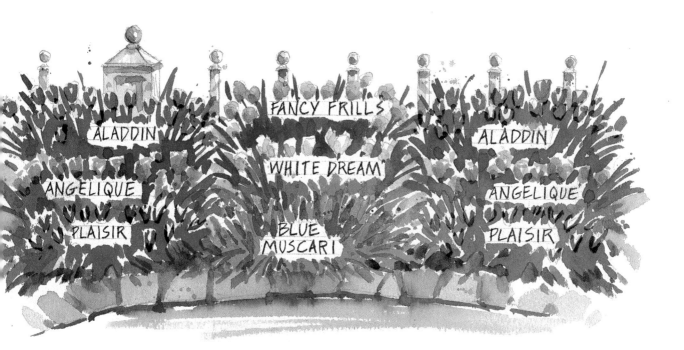

mixed border

This mixed tulip border contains a variety of April-blooming tulips with a central mass of dark blue muscari (grape hyacinth) for contrast. Taller varieties, such as the lily-flowered 'Aladdin' tulip, are placed in the back of the border, where they won't overshadow the shorter 'Plaisir' tulips. As you design your tulip garden, remember that a proper color scheme will bring out the best of every bulb you plant. Gardens that use a dominant color with a contrasting secondary color are most effective. Sometimes, if your

space is very limited, you may want to stick to a single color planted in masses scattered throughout the garden border. For example, above right, a small mass of 'Red Riding Hood' tulips transforms an ordinary garden path into a flower festival.

woodland border

Just when you think winter is never going to end, the spirit-lifting little bulbs burst into bloom. With shimmering jewellike flowers and bright green leaves, these reliable plants are especially welcome after a long, hard winter. They're all easy to grow, and once established, many species will spread quickly, lighting up the darkest corners of your landscape. In fact, many of these early birds actually prefer to grow under deciduous trees in a woodland site. In this border, early tulips, crocus, scilla, anemone, eranthis, and leucojum are massed in a protected location under a clump of white birch. Here they'll receive enough sunlight to bloom, but later in the season when the trees leaf out, the bulb foliage will be protected from hot weather. In the garden above left, 'Spring Beauty' scilla enjoys the rich, forest soil.

HOSTA
SIEBOLDIANA

BRIDAL VEIL
ASTILBE

HOSTA
SIEBOLDIANA

ZANTEDESCHIA

NONSTOP BEGONIAS

VIOLETS

VIOLETS

shady border

Bulbs and perennial flowers with shade-loving natures can work together to transform even the gloomiest garden into a work of art. In this border, perennial favorites such as hosta, astilbe, and violet are teamed with a mixed bag of bulbs. Both 'Non-stop' begonias and zantedeschia (calla lilies) offer colorful solutions for partially shady locations. In fact, tuberous begonias are available in so

many colors and flower forms, you almost can create an entire garden just with them. In the trial garden above right, you'll find just a sampling of tuberous begonia options. All shade plants benefit from rich, slightly moist soil and an occasional feeding with a liquid plant food. In northern gardens, the tuberous begonias and calla lilies need to be dug up and stored for the winter.

cutting border

Whether you want one big exuberant display for a special dinner party or just a stem or two in an old bottle or bud vase, it pays to raise your own cut flowers. Homegrown cut flowers cost little , and when you plant them right outside the kitchen door, you can have fresh bouquets as you need them. For summer flowers, you can't beat bulbs like gladiolus, lily, and dahlia. Once planted, all three grow quickly, producing armloads of wonderful cut flowers before you know it. Because each gladiolus bulb produces only one flower stalk, it's important to plant new crops of bulbs every two weeks through midsummer. In this garden, dahlias are planted in front of the gladiolus. That way, the dahlias keep the garden colorful as each set of gladiolus bulbs blooms and is harvested. Gladiolus, above left, and dahlias require winter storage in the North.

sunny border

In the heat of June and July, count on summer's indelible colors, ranging from sunny yellow hues to soothing pinks and blues. In this sunny border, the flame-red spikes of 'The President' cannas tower majestically over drifts of dwarf cannas, lilies, zantedeschia, and border dahlias. Bright yellow 'Grand Prix' dahlias flank the 'The President,' preventing the bright red flowers from becoming too overpowering. Up front, an army of mixed border dahlias keeps the garden in top form right up until the first frost. Asiatic hybrid lilies such as 'Dreamland' or 'Enchantment,' above, are at their best when they get at least six hours of direct sunlight a day. To avoid weeding and constant watering, keep your sunny border mulched at all times.

zone map

The key to successful gardening is knowing what plants are best suited to y our area and when to plant them. This is true for every type of gardening. Climate maps, such as the USDA Plant Hardiness Map of the United States and Canada, *opposite*, give a good idea of the extremes in temperature by zones. The zone-number listings tell you the coldest temperature a plant typically can endure.

 By choosing plants best adapted to the different zones, and by planting them at the right time, you will have many more successes.

The climate in your area is a mixture of many different weather patterns: sun, snow, rain, wind, and humidity. To be a good gardener, you should know, on the average, how cold the garden gets in winter, how much rainfall it receives each year, and how hot or dry it becomes in a typical summer. You can obtain this information from your state agricultural school or your county extension agent. In addition, acquaint yourself with the miniclimates in your neighborhood, based on such factors as wind protection gained from a nearby hill, or humidity and cooling offered by a local lake or river. Then carry the research further by studying the microclimates that characterize your own plot of ground.

key points to keep in mind:

1. Plants react to exposure. Southern and western exposures are sunnier and warmer than northern and eastern ones. Light conditions very greatly even in a small yard. Match your plants' needs to the correct exposure.

2. Wind can damage many plants, by either drying the soil or knocking over the fragile growth. Protect plants from both summer and winter winds to increase their odds of survival and to save yourself the time and energy of staking plants and watering more frequently.

3. Consider elevation, too, when selecting plants. Cold air sweeps down hills and rests in low areas. These frost pockets are fine for some plantings, deadly for others. Plant vegetation that prefers a warm environment on the tops or sides of hills, never at the bottom.

4. Use fences, the sides of buildings, shrubs, and trees to your advantage. Watch the play of shadows, the sweep of winds, and the flow of snowdrifts in winter. These varying situations are ideal for some plants, harmful to others. In short, always look for ways to make the most of everything your yard has to offer.

THE USDA PLANT HARDINESS MAP
OF NORTH AMERICA

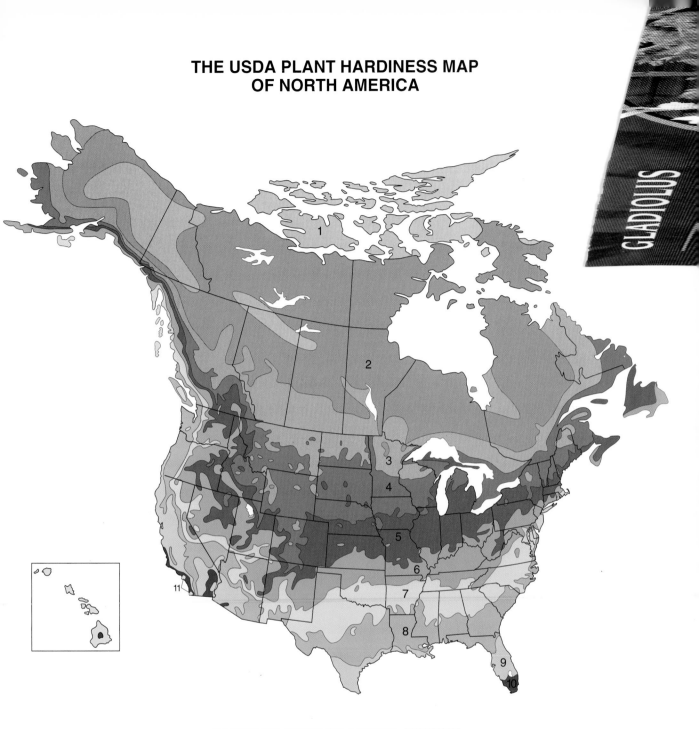

RANGE OF AVERAGE ANNUAL MINIMUM
TEMPERATURES FOR EACH ZONE

	ZONE 1	BELOW -50° F
	ZONE 2	-50° TO -40°
	ZONE 3	-40° TO -30°
	ZONE 4	-30° TO -20°
	ZONE 5	-20° TO -10°
	ZONE 6	-10° TO 0°
	ZONE 7	0° TO 10°
	ZONE 8	10° TO 20°
	ZONE 9	20° TO 30°
	ZONE 10	30° TO 40°
	ZONE 11	ABOVE 40°

resources

general bulbs

Daffodil Mart

Route 3, Box 794

Gloucester, VA 23061

(804) 693-3966

Dutch Gardens

P. O. Box 200

Adelphia, NJ 07710

(908) 780-2713

Jackson & Perkins

2518 S. Pacific Highway

Medford, OR 97501

(800) 292-4769

John Scheepers, Inc.

P.O. Box 700

Bantam, CT 06750

(203) 567-0838

K. Van Bourgondien

and Sons, Inc.

245 Farmingdale Road

P.O. Box 1000

Babylon, NY 11702-0598

(800) 552-9996

McClure & Zimmerman

P.O. Box 368

108 W. Winnebago

Friesland, WI 53935

Park Seed Co.

Cokesbury Road

Greenwood, SC 29647-0001

(800) 845-3366

Peter de Jager Bulb Co.

188 Asbury Street

P.O. Box 2010

South Hamilton, MA 01982

(508) 468-4707

Smith & Hawken

25 Corte Madera

Mill Valley, CA 94941-1829

(415) 383-2000

Van Dyck's Flower Farms

P.O. Box 430

Brightwaters, NY 11718-0430

(800) 248-2852

W. Atlee Burpee Co.

300 Park Avenue

Warminister, PA 18974

(215) 674-4900

Wayside Gardens

Hodges, SC 29695-0001

(800) 845-1124

White Flower Farm

P.O. Box 50

Litchfield, CT 06759-0050

(203) 496-9600

daffodils

Grant Mitsch Novelty Daffodils

P.O. Box 218

Hubbard, OR 97032

(503) 651-2742

Catalog: $3

Oregon Trail Daffodils

3207 S.E. Mannthey

Corbett, OR 97019

(503) 649-5513

dahlias

Swan Island Dahlias

P.O. Box 700

Canby, OR 97013

(503) 266-7711

gladiolus

Noweta Gardens

900 Whitewater Avenue

St. Charles, MN 55972

(507) 932-4859

hardy lilies

B & D Lilies

330 P Street

Port Townsend, WA 98368

(206) 385-1738

Catalog: $3

Borbeleta Gardens Inc.

15980 Canby Avenue

Faribault, MN 55021

(507) 334-2807

Catalog: $3

tools and supplies

de Van Koek

9400 Business Drive

Austin, TX 78758

(800) 992-1220

Gardener's Eden

P.O. Box 7307

San Francisco, CA 94120

(800) 822-9600

Gardener's Supply

128 Intervale Rd.

Burlington, VT 05401

(802) 863-1700

Kinsman Company

River Road

Point Pleasant, PA 18950

(800) 733-5613

Langenbach

P.O. Box 453

Blairstown, NJ 07825

(800) 362-1991

Smith & Hawken

25 Corte Madera

Mill Valley, CA 94941

(415) 383-2000

Snow & Nealley

P.O. Box 876

Bangor, ME 04402

(207) 947-6642

tools

Any job is easier with the right tools, and bulb planting is no exception. Here's a list of specialized tools that will make planting bulbs quick and painless. Invest in top-quality tools. You may pay more, but you'll have them longer.

dibble

An invaluable tool for planting bulbs, especially for little bulbs such as galanthus and crocus. A dibble allows you to make a hole to the depth you need, then, you can press in the bulb and cover it up. A dibble is the perfect tool for planting bulbs in hard-to-get-to areas, such as around rocks or in a rock wall.

garden fork

This tool allows you to dig a large area for planting bulbs in mass. To ensure drainage, use a garden fork to add sphagnum peat moss.

trowel

The standard tool of all gardeners, the trowel is a great bulb-planting tool. For larger bulbs, such as tulips and hyacinths, the trowel is the most efficient way of digging a small area for planting. For larger jobs, use a garden fork.

bulb auger

An ingenious tool that must have been invented by a bulb gardener, a bulb auger allows you to drill into the ground to the required depth for planting bulbs. Augers are available in different widths for different bulbs, and some attach to a power drill, to make the digging process almost effortless.

bulb planter

Able to cut through sod and soil with a single bound, bulb planters create the perfect hole for individual bulbs. For durability, choose one with a forged steel blade and a sturdy wooden handle.

For smaller jobs, use a hand-sized model. For bigger jobs, use a long-handled model with a foot tread so you can use your body weight rather than your back strength to dig a hole.

knee pads

You won't even feel the dampness of the cold earth when you use knee pads to plant your bulb garden. Since planting bulbs requires a lot of knee-breaking work, strap-on knee pads provide comfort, protection, and mobility.

flower cans

Cut flowers stay fresh as you're gathering your bouquet if you drop them into a water-filled flower can. Useful for gathering and transporting your cut blossoms, flower cans can be interesting enough to serve as rustic vases. Flower cans come in several heights.

garden cart

Useful in all types of gardening, garden carts transport tools, bulbs, and soil amendments

index